19.95

Implementing
Public Policy

Implementing Public Policy

WITHDRAWN

Edited by
Dennis J. Palumbo
Marvin A. Harder
The University of Kansas

LexingtonBooks
D.C. Heath and Company
Lexington, Massachusetts
Toronto

Library of Congress Cataloging in Publication Data
Main entry under title:

Implementing public policy.

1. Evaluation research (Social action programs)–Addresses, essays,
lectures. 2. Policy sciences–Addresses, essays, lectures. I. Palumbo, Dennis James, 1929–   II. Harder, Marvin Andrew, 1921–
H61.I516   361.6'1   80-8597
ISBN 0-669-04305-2

Copyright © 1981 by D.C. Heath and Company

Published simultaneously in Canada

Printed in the United States of America

International Standard Book Number: 0-669-04305-2

Library of Congress Catalog Card Number: 80-8597

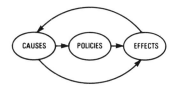

Policy Studies Organization Series

General Approaches to Policy Studies

81-1002

Specific Policy Problems

Analyzing Poverty Policy
  edited by Dorothy Buckton James
Crime and Criminal Justice
  edited by John A. Gardiner and Michael Mulkey
Civil Liberties
  edited by Stephen L. Wasby
Foreign Policy Analysis
  edited by Richard L. Merritt
Economic Regulatory Policies
  edited by James E. Anderson
Political Science and School Politics
  edited by Samuel K. Gove and Frederick M. Wirt
Science and Technology Policy
  edited by Joseph Haberer
Population Policy Analysis
  edited by Michael E. Kraft and Mark Schneider
The New Politics of Food
  edited by Don F. Hadwiger and William P. Browne
New Dimensions to Energy Policy
  edited by Robert Lawrence
Race, Sex, and Policy Problems
  edited by Marian Lief Palley and Michael Preston
American Security Policy and Policy-Making
  edited by Robert Harkavy and Edward Kolodziej
Current Issues in Transportation Policy
  edited by Alan Altshuler
Security Policies of Developing Countries
  edited by Edward Kolodziej and Robert Harkavy
Determinants of Law-Enforcement Policies
  edited by Fred A. Meyer, Jr., and Ralph Baker
Evaluating Alternative Law-Enforcement Policies
  edited by Ralph Baker and Fred A. Meyer, Jr.
International Energy Policy
  edited by Robert M. Lawrence and Martin O. Heisler
Employment and Labor-Relations Policy
  edited by Charles Bulmer and John L. Carmichael, Jr.
Housing Policy for the 1980s
  edited by Roger Montgomery and Dale Rogers Marshall
Environmental Policy Formation
  edited by Dean E. Mann
Environmental Policy Implementation
  edited by Dean E. Mann
The Analysis of Judicial Reform
  edited by Philip L. Dubois
The Politics of Judicial Reform
  edited by Philip L. Dubois
Critical Issues in Health Policy
  edited by Ralph Straetz, Marvin Lieberman, and Alice Sardell

Contents

                Design: Methods from a Formative Evaluation
                of the Florida Linkage System
                Garrett R. Foster and *Peter A. Easton*   119

Chapter 11   Optimizing Child-Welfare Policy through Research
                and Demonstration Projects   *Lenore Olsen*   129

Chapter 12   Pursuing Policy Optimization by Evaluating
                Implementation: Notes on the State of the Art
                James D. Sorg   139

                Indexes   155

                List of Contributors   167

                About the Editors   169

Introduction

In their seminal work on implementation, Pressman and Wildavsky reproduce several Rube Goldberg cartoons depicting a complicated sequence of steps that have to be taken in order to produce a specific outcome (Pressman and Wildavsky, 1973). One of them shows no fewer than seventeen separate events that must occur (each of which may go awry) in order for one to turn the pages of sheet music for someone who is playing the violin. The implication of the several cartoons is that there must be a better way to turn sheet music pages, or to implement public policy, because policies are sure to go wrong when they must cover complicated and treacherous grounds, such as those in the jobs program in Oakland, California, described by Pressman and Wildavsky.

But did the jobs program in Oakland really fail? It is difficult to answer this, for Pressman and Wildavsky gave no explicit criteria for determining what a successful program would have been. In fact, it is not possible to determine when public policies succeed, for success and failure, as Ingram and Mann (1980) note, are slippery concepts that cannot be easily defined.

When Pressman and Wildavsky wrote their book in the early 1970s, they noted that there had been very little research on implementation and that there was no theory of implementation. Since their book was published in 1973, there has been an explosion of research on the subject but still no great advances toward the development of a theory on it.

Policy implementation, Edwards writes, "is the stage of policy making between the establishment of a policy—such as the passage of a legislative act, the issuing of an executive order, the handing down of a judicial decision, or the promulgation of a regulatory rule—and the consequences of the policy for the people whom it affects" (Edwards, 1980, p. 1). This indeed covers a large territory that, for the most part, is unknown and unexplored. We know something about the factors that affect implementation, such as communications, resources, self-interests, and bureaucratic structure (Edwards, 1980; Nakamura and Smallwood, 1980). But we know very little about the extremely wide range of tools that the government can use in implementing policy and how these are related to successful implementation (Salamon, 1980; Bardach, 1980). And, although we have more than half a century of research in public administration, we know very little about the administrative conditions under which we might expect given policy goals to be faithfully implemented. In fact, the traditional way of understanding public administration is likely to impede rather than help us understand implementation.

We now know that two of the assumptions of traditional public administration are incorrect. One is that policy is made by legislators and carried out by administrators, and the other is that the directives of top-level administrators should be carried out by lower-level people in the organization exactly as those at the top (for example, management) intend. We have known for some time that administrators make policy. Also, we now know that policy is made by all parts of the hierarchy of administrative agencies, including street-level bureaucrats, not just by those at the top. In fact, the extent of involvement in policy-making by street-level bureaucrats has caused us to stand the study of public policy implementation on its head (Lipsky, 1978).

Thus, although we know some things about implementation, huge gaps remain in our knowledge. At the heart of the matter is the question of how much change should occur in policy during implementation. A great deal of contemporary research about implementation seems to accept the traditional model of public administration when it defines successful and unsuccessful implementation in terms of goal-directed behavior. For example, Sabatier and Mazmanian (1979) write that for implementation to be successful, the goals of policy must be clearly stated so as to give clear directives to administrators who have to implement the policy. In the same vein, Edwards writes that "confusion by implementors about what to do increases the chances that they will not implement a policy as those who passed it or ordered it intended" (Edwards, 1980, p. 10).

The problem with these views is that they make unrealistic assumptions about the legislative and administrative processes. First, legislators do not usually provide clear goals when they pass laws. They have to satisfy diverse constituencies in order to get sufficient support for a policy, and they can best do this if the goals of the policy are stated in broad and vague terms. Second, organizations do not follow a top-down model in the sense that all the lower-echelon members do precisely what those at the top "order." There is inevitably a large degree of discretion at all levels of an organization, and this is not always used to implement the interpretation those at the top have of the policy goals.

Successful implementation occurs in an evolutionary way. The somewhat vague goals stated in legislation are interpreted by administrators as they begin to implement the policy. This interpretation is amplified as the policy filters down the organizational hierarchy. At the end of the process what actually is implemented is quite different from the original interpretations and may often be at variance with them. Policies are changed to fit the needs and standard operating procedures of the agencies and individuals that carry them out (Allison, 1971). They are implemented so as to produce as little disruption as possible to existing agreements, coalitions, power, and status in an organization. This almost invariably requires many adjustments in the policy during the process of implementation.

The changes that occur in public policy during implementation are not necessarily bad. They occur because implementing agencies and individuals have a great deal of autonomy and discretion. The autonomy of state and local governments in the federal system enables them to adapt policy to local needs. As a result, many beneficial changes are made in policies when they are implemented through the federal government (Weatherly, 1980, p. 10). If successful implementation means carrying out goals exactly as they are specified by top-level legislators and administrators, then there can be no discretion at the middle and lower levels in an organization. For example, Edwards writes that "inadequate communication also provides implementors with discretion as they attempt to turn general policies into specific actions. This discretion will not necessarily be exercised to further the aims of the original decision makers" (Edwards, 1980, p. 10). Are we to assume from this that discretion should not exist? One would hope not, because discretion at lower levels is not only inevitable, but also desirable. It may provide the flexibility that is needed to turn a poorly conceived and badly designed policy into something that is relatively successful. It is necessary for policies to be "reinvented" so that they better fit local needs (Rice and Rogers, 1980).

Perhaps what is considered to be bad is not the fact that changes in policy occur during implementation but that, in such cases, administrators make policy. This could lead to undesirable consequences when administrators collaborate with local power elites or when regulatory agencies become dominated by those they are supposed to regulate, in which case those benefiting from a policy may not be the ones intended by the legislators. This occurred to some degree in urban renewal and housing programs in this country; the middle class rather than the poor often benefited. In these cases we might assume that administrative discretion should be checked. But because it may be abused at times does not mean that administrative discretion should not exist at all. The problem with administrative discretion is that in the American political system there are no guidelines for determining how administrators should make policy. There are well-defined procedures that legislators must follow in making policy, but none for administrative agencies. There are no provisions for voting and representation in administrative policymaking. Except for recent developments, such as ombudsmen and legislative post audit, there is no systematic means for citizens to appeal decisions of administrators or for replacing the administrators when they make policy decisions people do not like.

Changes made in policy during implementation might therefore be considered illegitimate. This, perhaps, is the main reason why there is a tendency to define successful implementation as occurring only when policy goals are carried out. But this puts us right back in line with the traditional model of public administration that does not allow any leakage, drift, shifts, or changes in policies during implementation. This is unrealistic administratively, for it is not possible to get complete and absolute compliance with goals that are set by top-level administrators. It also is unrealistic in a practical sense because often a policy must be changed in order to have it carried out at all.

A theory of implementation must be able to explain the changes that occur in a policy during implementation. In an attempt to do this, Berman (1980) differentiates between programmed and adaptive implementation, arguing that only under certain limited conditions should we expect policies to remain static during implementation. Another useful way to conceptualize implementation is found in the work on innovation by Rice and Rogers (1980). They distinguish between planned and reactive reinvention of innovation during implementation. *Planned implementation* occurs when changes are expected as a part of the implementation process and provision is made for them. *Reactive implementation* is when changes occur because of unexpected consequences encountered during implementation.

A theory of implementation also must explain the stages that occur during implementation. Rice and Rogers's stages concerning the reinvention process for innovations are useful in understanding this aspect of implementation. These stages are agenda setting, matching, redefining, structuring, and interconnecting. These explain how an innovation (that is, policy) is changed during implementation. Once a policy is put on the agenda, it is inspected to see if it will help solve a problem being faced by an agency (matching); then it is redefined to fit the agency's needs. If these stages are completed successfully, the agency will be restructured to accommodate the policy. Finally, the policy becomes part of the standard operating procedure of the agency.

A theory of implementation also needs to include mechanisms the government uses to carry out public policy (Salamon, 1980; Bardach, 1980). These include issuing directives, making loans, signing contracts, and many other devices. No good typology exists concerning these many different tools or technologies. We know that how a policy is implemented is related to the kind of implementation tool used. How well a policy is implemented and what its consequence or impact is depends on whether government carries out a policy through its own agencies, such as the Tennessee Valley Authority (TVA), or whether it relies on private business organizations, as it did in urban renewal.

The principal method used to study implementation is the case study. Case studies do not lend themselves to broad theoretical generalizations, but they do often point to factors that must be considered in the development of a theory. This book does not present a theory of policy implementation nor does it attempt to cover all the issues related to implementation. Instead, it focuses on a central theme, the one developed in the larger policy studies symposium from which this book was extracted. The symposium contained a sufficiently large number of good papers to justify publishing two separate books: this one and one titled *Evaluating and Optimizing Public Policy*. The books go hand in hand because they both are based on the same theme: policies invariably will be changed during implementation and this has significant implications for evaluating and optimizing them. In this book we look at the kinds of changes that are likely to occur during implementation, the conditions that lead to these changes, and how implementation can be improved through evaluation.

Robert T. Nakamura and Dianne M. Pinderhughes, in "Changing Anacostia: Definition and Implementation," have provided their readers with four conclusions derived from their study of the history of federally supported school projects in the Anacostia region of the District of Columbia and an analysis based on three well-known scenarios: (1) agreement through mutual adjustment around common goals, (2) agreement through bargaining over diverse goals, and (3) agreement imposed through the authoritative use of political power. It is their purpose to clarify the difficulties involved when policymakers decided to leave the definition of policy to those charged with implementation and to specify the political strategies used to achieve a definition of policy. This chapter is presented first because of its succinct introduction to implementation issues. Beyond that its utility lies in the authors' ability to put in bold relief the consequences that can occur when a policymaker fails to define either the policy he wants implemented or the means by which he wants that policy achieved (that is, to meet the conditions of a hypothesis as specified by Pressman and Wildavsky).

Guenther Kress, Gustav Koehler, and J. Fred Springer create the concept *policy drift* as a means of identifying how changes occurred in a California program to assist the blind. In their chapter they conclude that the policy changes resulted from an accumulation of specific decisions made without an articulated intent to change the policy. The term *drift* illustrates a kind of change in policy that is different from what is described in other chapters in this section. They found that evaluations, rather than administrators, propelled the drift.

In "Organizational Goals and Their Impact on the Policy Implementation Process," George E. Rawson reconstructs the history of decision making in the Tennessee Valley Authority with respect to its power program. Beginning with a somewhat ambiguous, multigoal mandate, TVA commissioners eventually made a policy decision to generate electrical power, first by means of coal and then by nuclear generating plants. Successful implementation followed a resolution of these goal issues. In his analysis of the case, the author finds support for five propositions that relate goals to implementation. In general, the propositions lend support to the idea that successful implementation may be more likely when an organization is relatively unfettered by a legislative policy mandate and is therefore free to define its goals and select the means of achieving them. This thesis runs counter to the premise in many implementation studies that legislative policy ambiguity is a prime cause of implementation failure.

The number of problems faced by an agency trying to implement policies is enormous. We have selected only a few in the next section of the book. James A. Goodrich deals with the implementation difficulties encountered in the Comprehensive Employment and Training Act (CETA) program. He identifies five problem areas that hinder optimal implementation of the program. He also discusses the likelihood that the current attempts to improve CETA performance by tightening federal control of program resources will succeed. As Goodrich sees it, these efforts are off target. CETA's prime sponsors exercise considerable discretion in executing CETA policies, and it is at this point that efforts to improve CETA should be focused. More attention should be paid to improving local staff performance than to increasing controls over program resources. Goodrich's conclusion supports the notion in the implementation literature that program administrators, through their exercise of authority and discretion, are the most powerful variable for explaining implementation success or failure.

The deinstitutionalization of chronically handicapped individuals, the subject of Beryce W. MacLennan's chapter, "Political Power and Policy Formulation, Implementation, and Evaluation," is an example of what can happen when a change in technology is adopted and the dislocations and disturbances that are likely to accompany that change have not been considered. The failure in strategic planning that the author illustrates is shocking because the consequences described were so predictable. MacLennan's prescription, "work out a careful strategy before attempting to implement a technological change," is an appropriate contribution to the literature of implementation.

Delay in implementation was one of the principal problems found by Pressman and Wildavsky in the Oakland program. Delay usually is considered dysfunctional, but, as Marvin Harder shows in the case of water-quality standards in Kansas, delay can sometimes be functional. In fact, since policy evolves while it is being implemented, delays may provide the time needed to improve or adapt policy to local circumstances.

The next section of the book reflects the growing awareness among policy analysts and program evaluators that effective program evaluation is intrinsically related to the implementation process. In "On the Hazards of Selecting Intervention Points: Time-Series Analysis of Mandated Policies," Michael C. Musheno discusses the problems of determining the initial implementation point for public policies—a necessary precondition for effective evaluations using time-series analysis. The difficulty, as Musheno sees it, stems from the current lack of an implementation theory that tells us when implementation actually has occurred. The time taken between policy adoption and actual program implementation, Musheno terms *implementation lag.*

The next chapter, like Musheno's, suggests a means of improving program evaluation by attending more closely to the implementation process. In " 'Patching Up' Evaluation Designs: The Case for Process Evaluation," John Clayton Thomas notes the difficulties encountered in traditional outcome evaluations. Thomas suggests combining outcome evaluation with implementation assessment techniques and monitoring the level of program activities.

Elaine B. Sharp suggests that the kind of evaluation that should be done depends on what model of implementation is being used. If we assume that the classical top-down administrative model is the appropriate one, then the appropriate type of evaluation is summative evaluation. On the other hand, in most real-world situations, such as the one in Midtown that she describes, an adaptive implementation strategy is more appropriate.

In the final section of the book, Garrett Foster and Peter Easton's chapter, "Dealing with Changes in a Program's Goals and Design: Methods from a

Formative Evaluation of the Florida Linkage System," suggests a way of improving implementation through evaluation. The authors outline a formative evaluation procedure for use during implementation for "adjusting the official objectives and methods" of a program "to the changing reality of the project and the changing perceptions of those involved." Successful implementation depends, they argue, on the degree to which mutual adaptation takes place between a program and those responsible for implementation.

One of the principal things that occurs during implementation is that goals are redefined to more accurately reflect the changed relationships between the organization and its environment. Leonore Olsen's chapter shows that the placement of children in foster-care homes was improved when evaluators focused on goals that emerged during implementation and fed this information into the decision-making process.

In the final chapter of this book, James D. Sorg describes two types of implementation evaluation: implementation monitoring, which involves collecting data about the processes of macro- and micro-implementation, and program documentation, which refers to impact evaluation. If both are done, we are not likely to make the mistake of evaluating a program that never was implemented. Also, an impact evaluation will not be done prematurely. Some programs—community correction in Kansas is a good example—take a very long time to be implemented. An impact evaluation of such a program is likely to be misleading.

In summary, the chapters, if treated as representative of the implementation literature, suggest the fluidity of thinking today about the conditions that affect implementation successes and failures. In this formative stage in the development of implementation theory, a consensus has not yet evolved. It is too early to predict whether scholars and practitioners will ever agree on a single, preferred strategy by which implementation failures can be avoided. It is difficult to be hopeful as long as we remain uncertain about the criteria by which policies and programs should be evaluated.

References

Allison, Graham. *Essence of Decision.* Boston: Little, Brown, 1971.

Bardach, Eugene. "Implementation Studies and the Study of Implements." Paper prepared for delivery at the 1980 annual meeting of the American Political Science Association.

Berman, Paul. "Thinking about Programmed and Adaptive Implementation: Matching Strategies to Situations." In *Why Policies Succeed or Fail,* edited by Helen M. Ingram and Dean Mann. Beverly Hills: Sage Publications, 1980.

Edwards, George C. *Implementing Public Policy.* Washington, D.C.: Congressional Quarterly Press, 1980.

Ingram, Helen M., and Mann, Dean. *Why Policies Succeed or Fail.* Vol. 8. Sage

Yearbooks in Politics and Public Policy. Beverly Hills: Sage Publications, 1980.

Lipsky, Michael "Standing the Study of Public Policy Implementation on Its Head." In *American Politics and Public Policy,* edited by W.D. Burnham and M.W. Weinberg. Cambridge, Mass.: MIT Press, 1978.

Nakamura, Robert, and Smallwood, Frank. *The Politics of Policy Implementation.* New York: St. Martin's Press, 1980.

Palumbo, Dennis, ed. "Optimizing, Implementing and Evaluating Public Policy," *Policy Studies Journal* 8, no. 7 (1980).

Pressman, Jeffrey L., and Wildavsky, Aaron B. *Implementation.* Berkeley: University of California Press, 1973.

Rice, Ronald E., and Rogers, Everett. "Reinvention and the Innovation Process," *Knowledge* 1(1980):499–515.

Sabatier, Paul, and Mazmanian, Daniel. "The Conditions of Effective Implementation: A Guide to Accomplishing Policy Objectives." *Policy Analysis* (Fall 1979):481–504.

Salamon, Lester. "Rethinking Implementation." Paper prepared for delivery at the 1980 annual meeting of the American Political Science Association.

Weatherley, Richard. "Implementing Social Programs: The View from the Front Line." Paper prepared for delivery at the 1980 annual meeting of the American Political Science Association.

Part I
Redefining Policy during Implementation

1

Changing Anacostia: Definition and Implementation

Robert T. Nakamura and
Dianne M. Pinderhughes

Introduction

This is a history and analysis of federal educational projects in the Anacostia area of the District of Columbia from 1967 to 1977. Specifically, we describe origins and development of the Anacostia Community School Project (1967-1972) and its successor, the Response to Educational Needs Project (1972-1977). These projects—administered by the United States Office of Education and later the National Institute of Education—were intended to improve schooling in a troubled, low-income, black area through community participation and other means. Our data are drawn from interviews with participants and from documents and records contained in the files of the projects, federal educational agencies, and private organizations.[1]

Our work has three main purposes. First, we want to describe what happened and why. Second, we want to arrive at some general conclusions about the Anacostia experience, placing it within the context of general implementation problems. Third, we want to isolate the lessons Anacostia holds for policymakers contemplating alternative strategies to improve education. After an introduction orienting the reader to the location of this study within the implementation literature, the remainder of this chapter is divided according to our substantive areas of concern: history, analysis, and lessons.

Studying Implementation

The literature on policy implementation is a new and growing one. While particular case studies of governmental programs have been with us for some time, the explicit focus on "implementation" as a research perspective has not. This literature is new because it addresses a common core of policy questions through the adoption of common perspective. The major and distinctive concern of implementation research is to produce prescriptive, or policy-relevant, studies.

This study was supported by a contract administered by Gibboney Associates from the National Institutes of Education (NIE). The work reflects the conclusions of the authors only, and is not endorsed by Gibboney Associates or the NIE in any way.

3

An assumption of implementation researchers is that their findings are relevant across the traditional boundaries of case-specific subject areas. Thus, the students of implementation engage in a dialogue that assumes that the experience of a jobs program in Oakland (Pressman, 1973) is relevant to laws on mental commitment in California (Bardach, 1977) and Health, Education, and Welfare (HEW) school desegregation efforts in Washington and the nation (Radin, 1978). This dialogue clarifies the problems policymakers encounter in trying to improve the delivery of services through intermediaries.

The study of implementation also involves the problem of evaluating the success of officials in "translating broad agreement into specific decisions, given a wide range of participants and perspectives" (Pressman and Wildavsky, 1973). The degree to which those goals are actually achieved through specific decisions, then, is the test of the degree of implementation achieved.

The initial difficulty in studying implementation is, then, defining the policy being implemented: defining what it is that the policymaker hopes to achieve and how. Pressman and Wildavsky (1973) state the dictionary definition of implementation as "to carry out, accomplish, fulfill, produce, complete." They proceed to define the policy being carried out, accomplished, and produced in specific enough terms to sustain analysis. This is an essential first step. The intent of policymakers should be specific enough to constitute a baseline against which success or failure can be measured. Measuring implementation, in this view, is akin to measuring political power: we must know the goals of the initiator of implementation or of the person reputed to be powerful, before we estimate its success or failure.

Despite the prevalence of such means-ends language, particularly in federal evaluator circles, there are real problems with that view. The difficulty is that complex policies often do not lend themselves to clear statements about which of a policymaker's general or proximate goals is being implemented. Often policymakers state their goals in vague and imprecise forms. Policymakers may know generally what they hope to achieve—less pollution, illiteracy, unemployment—but they are not certain how goals should be achieved or at what price. In policy areas like the environment, education, and the economy, this problem is exacerbated by uncertainties arising out of complex social, organizational, and political environments (Rein and Rabinowitz, 1978).[2]

The difficulty in finding clear statements of goals and means for any large-scale governmental policy—not just implementation of new policies—has been repeatedly encountered. The debate over Planning, Programming, Budgeting Systems (PPBS) turned on the inability of analysts to formulate specific goals acceptable to politicians and bureaucrats against which expenditures could be measured (Wildavsky, 1966; Sullivan, Nakamura, and Winters, 1980). Charles Lindblom (1979) argued that this confusion about goals stemmed from the incremental method of decision making in which agreement on goals was typically not secured prior to the adoption of a specific policy.

Theodore Lowi (1969) analyzes American national policy making in terms consistent with Lindblom. He argues that national policymakers typically state goals in rather vague and abstract terms. Then these policymakers—Congress and the president—grant legislative discretion and resources to others, usually governmental agencies, to further define these goals by devising the specific means to carry them out. This process of definition is characterized by bargaining and adjustments between the governmental agencies and attentive publics of interest groups that will be affected by the resulting policies. Appeals from this process can be made back up to political decision makers or carried through the courts. This approach seems to be most common in areas where goals can be stated clearly in the abstract—end discrimination based on race, sex, physical handicaps; clean up the air, water or land—but whose achievement may be technically or politically complex.

The Anacostia case is an example of a project whose implementation began before policy was designed as a specific statement of ends and means. Our work is not a conventional implementation study; it does not compare the project's accomplishments against the prescriptions and goals of the policy. Our contribution is in clarifying the difficulties involved when policymakers decide to leave the definition of policy to those charged with implementation, and in specifying the political strategies used to achieve a definition of policy.

Studying Anacostia

The history of the Anacostia projects will not sustain an implementation study in the conventional sense of evaluating the degree to which a change initially posited by policymakers was achieved or not achieved. President Johnson's initial proposal outlined vague and abstract goals and did not specify the means for achieving them. The more specific goals—developed by community participants, federal agencies, and congressional staff during the course of the projects—were objects of controversy rather than consensus. Common goals existed—to improve education in Anacostia—but these were often stated at so high a level of abstraction that agreement was not meaningful.

There were also divergences among the goals of the various community, local, and federal participants. Community participants became committed to the community control themes current in the 1960s. Federal actors, over time, became committed to the educational management and experiment themes of the early 1970s: management by objectives requiring the identification of specific goals and means, as well as stress on the production of evaluable results. Finally, local school officials and others came to emphasize the "back to basics" themes of the late 1970s.

Such specific goal differences were not the only sources of conflict over preferred policies. The implementation of the project itself altered the organizational environment in which policy alternatives were considered. An apparatus for community participation was created before the policy was defined, and this community body became an important focus for project energies. A new political unit was founded in a poor community where none had existed before, and it created the resources to articulate demands unanticipated by policymakers and their agents. In addition, the community organization became concerned with its own maintenance.

So, because of conflicts in participant preferences about goals and means, and the existence of organizations capable of sustaining differences in the face of challenges, differences in policy had to be resolved through politics. In this chapter we will concentrate on the political lessons of the Anacostia experience. Our colleague, Dr. Bruce Cooper, deals elsewhere with the educational innovations spawned by the projects (Cooper, 1978).

A Summary of Conclusions on the Anacostia Experience

First Conclusion

The conventional conception of policy making and policy implementation is inappropriate for understanding the history of the Anacostia school projects.

The Conventional Model: Without going into detail, the elements of the conventional conception of policy making and policy implementation present the process as a bounded and sequential one. There are clear boundaries between the roles played by policymakers (usually elected officials) and policy implementers. These boundaries are established by a clear and sequential division of labor between policymakers who set goals and specify the means for implementing them and the policy implementers who carry out that policy.[3]

For this to happen, policymakers have to achieve some final consensus among themselves on goals, and they must have sufficient information as to the means of achieving those goals. Policy implementers, for their part, are given clear direction by policymakers and are assumed to have both the technical capacity and will necessary to carry out policymakers' directives.

The conventional model has a number of things to recommend it as a guide to research. First, it is concerned with the ways in which the goals of legitimate officials are translated into action by bureaucrats and others in the permanent structure of government. Second, the model prescribes the order in which implementation research should be organized, beginning with the policy making, proceeding to implementation, and concluding with an evaluation of how well or how poorly the original policy goals were satisfied. Third, by positing policy goals at the outset, the model provides researchers with objective criteria for conducting an evaluation of the success or failure of the implementation process.

Anacostia Does Not Fit the Policy Definition Model: The history of the Anacostia projects does not follow the pattern of the conventional model. Policy
was not definitively stated; instead, policymakers concentrated their attention
on short-run goals achieved by the initial input of resources into Anacostia with
little attention to specific long-term goals; policy implementers did not press
for a clarification of policy prior to implementation; policy making and policy
implementation occurred simultaneously and continued on an open-ended basis
for the duration of the project.

In this case, President Johnson and his White House staff concentrated on
immediate problems: maintain civil order in the District of Columbia (fear of
riots); show movement and action on the problems of urban education in the
District and elsewhere (advance the War on Poverty); demonstrate the effectiveness of the Great Society in order to build political credit for the upcoming 1968
election. Proximate goals had to be accomplished within the constraints imposed
by limited resources, the need to get started quickly, and the bureaucratic and
organizational limitations of the District of Columbia Public Schools (DCPS).

Announcing an experimental project in a few Washington schools, whose
characteristics were to be defined by community participants as well as District
and federal educational authorities, solved immediate problems but left both the
means and long-term goals for policy implementers to determine. Because com-
paratively small resources ($10 million promised) were focused on a limited
number of Washington schools, the prospects for dramatic results from limited
resources were enhanced.

The White House also avoided the complex and potentially time-consuming
problem of specifying means in an uncertain and difficult policy area. By sketching out a new political arena—whose participants included community residents,
federal and local school officials—the White House believed it was avoiding the
difficulties associated with the strife-torn District of Columbia Public Schools.
Finally, the general goal of improving urban education nationally—by developing and proving techniques in a limited number of District schools—could be
made consistent with the input of limited resources promised in the Johnson plan.

Long-term goals and the means of achieving them were left vague because
policymakers were uncertain about what should be accomplished and how.
White House policymakers behaved in ways inconsistent with the prescriptions
of the conventional conception of policy making.

Anacostia Does Not Fit the Policy Implementation Model: Policy implementers—
initially the U.S. Office of Education (USOE) and District of Columbia Public
Schools—had few initial incentives to press the White House for more precise
policy instructions, since they considered themselves more competent than the
White House on the subject of urban education. The vagueness of White House
directives constituted a resource for the implementers, giving them considerable
discretion in spending promised new money. So, for a variety of reasons, policy

implementers accepted the unconventional role of policymaker as an adjunct to their conventional role as policy implementer.

Second Conclusion

The first step in the implementation process—the creation of a local arena to define and implement policy—occurred prior to the definition of policy.

Since the Johnson White House did not clearly specify the policy to be implemented, federal and local educational authorities were given discretion to do so. The first task of policy implementation was the creation of an arena for the definition of policy.

In a series of joint actions, the USOE and DCPS identified the Anacostia area as the recipient of the project, and identified the community as the locus of policy definition and proposed governance. Neither the USOE nor DCPS considered it its job to propose a new comprehensive plan—specifying the relationships between means and ends—on the community.

The USOE initially avoided the role of planner because Congress had previously expressed concern over federal influence in education; several USOE officials (including the commissioner, the bureau chief, and a project officer) believed that community participants should be given primary responsibility for directing and defining the project; and no consensus existed among professional educators as to the most appropriate remedies for urban educational ills.

The DCPS avoided a role as central planner because it was only a nominal conduit for federal money; Anacostia residents held the DCPS in low repute; and the DCPS administrator most involved with Anacostia had goals consistent with community concerns (for example, inservice training of teachers, the use of community residents as aides, and so on).

Although community residents were given the discretion to plan both means and goals and to implement them, they were formally constrained by federal and local educational authorities. These constraints became significant when the leadership of the USOE changed (as the Johnson administration was replaced by Nixon's) and when the DCPS was called on to circumvent its normal administrative procedures to implement project goals. The community held the initial right to define specific goals and means, but this right could only be effectively exercised with the approval of the USOE and DCPS. When one or both withdrew their approval, the developing Anacostia leadership sought to reduce the consequences of USOE-DCPS action through political efforts. This will be discussed in the next section.

Third Conclusion

The Anacostia community arena developed its own agenda of concerns separate from those of either federal or local educational authorities. By using federal resources, as well as developing political resources of their own, Anacostia participants gained a degree of independence from both federal and local educational authorities.

The USOE-DCPS decision to create and fund a local intermediary produced a locally-based and locally-organized constituency with priorities independent of those who had created it.

The original plan required that the White House provide the political support in Congress needed to get federal resources for improving education in Washington; that federal and District officials identify a geographic setting for the project and to provide technical help; that community participants identify a more specific set of goals and plan a structure for their achievement; and that a locally-run educational staff implement those goals in an efficient fashion. Participants at this stage assumed that voluntary cooperation, coordinated by common goals, would be sufficient to produce a functioning program in short order.

These expectations did not come to pass. Congress proved less cooperative than the Johnson administration had anticipated. After initially refusing to fund the project at all, Congress—in response to White House and Anacostia community pressures—provided a fraction of the money originally requested. The initially broad educational plan written by community participants had to be drastically trimmed. But many of the expectations about what the project should do did not diminish along with the money, and these remained to plague participants who preferred to reduce resources devoted to many goals rather than to reduce the total number of goals and focus resources.

Over time, the Anacostia-based participants became even more active in securing and protecting their sources of congressional support. After the Johnson administration was replaced by that of Nixon, Anacostia was able to develop allies on Capitol Hill, and the project succeeded in having many of its succeeding appropriations "earmarked" by the Senate Labor-HEW Appropriations Subcommittee. This, of course, reduced Anacostia's sense of dependence on federal education agencies and on District school officials. Anacostians came to believe that the project was theirs to control and to change.

One sign of this growing sense of independence from federal agencies was the Anacostia Community School Board's assumption of administrative as well as policymaking responsibilities. As the local participants became committed to the goal of community control, the board asserted greater discretion in changing project goals as well as in controlling staff activities.

In addition, membership on the Anacostia boards became a source of material and status rewards for community residents. These boards became the legitimate representative of the community in its dealings with outside authorities in the federal and District of Columbia governments, the principal policy and administrative body for running project activities within Anacostia schools, and a sounding board for local concerns.

These and other developments helped to define the difficulties the Anacostia boards were to encounter. There were internal political conflicts in

Anacostia—evidenced by frequent contested elections and board splits—over the distribution of project resources, a conflict made worse by the many legitimate goals that existed. In addition, the boards found themselves at odds with District school authorities when inexperienced community residents—in their efforts to run the project—had to cope with the bureaucratic intricacies of District hiring and supply-acquisition practices. But the most serious conflicts were between Anacostia and federal educational authorities. When the USOE personnel who were favorable to community control were replaced by Nixon appointees and others, these problems came to a head. Eventually the USOE concluded that the Anacostia project had performed its educational planning and administrative functions poorly, and the USOE decided to terminate the project.

By this point, however, the Anacostia project had developed its ideology of community control and had built a core of community supporters based on the material and status rewards it conferred. These core activists mobilized community supporters and took their case to Capitol Hill where shared values and the perception of common enemies (the Nixon administration) helped them defeat attempts by the USOE to terminate the project. Consequently, Congress gave responsibility for the Anacostia project to the National Institutes of Education (NIE) and federal-local conflicts continued in another specific relationship.

Fourth Conclusion

The main problem encountered by participants (community, local, and federal) was a persistent inability to agree on a common policy for the project to implement.

The community, city, and federal participants were unable to settle on a single definitive policy throughout most of the project's duration. Major participants had different preferences concerning goals and means. There were shortcomings in leadership. And there were changes in the organizational priorities of participants over time.

All participants—federal, city, and local—might agree that improving the education of Anacostia children was an important goal, but there was no real agreement among the participants on what to work for, how to work for it, and how to evaluate the results. A second factor explaining the inability to agree was turnover in leadership within the various organizations participating in the Anacostia negotiations. Each set of leaders brought in a different set of expectations and preferences about Anacostia, without a full understanding of the project's history; leadership turnover thus produced a confounding effect on the negotiation process.[4]

During this lengthy process, the organizational priorities of participants changed. The Anacostia project came into being as an organization, and quickly developed a stake in its continued survival. What had begun as a series of community meetings was transformed into an important actor in its own right. The DCPS also changed its overall direction several times, moving from a narrow emphasis on reading and mathematics in the Clark plan (Superintendent Scott) to decentralization (Superintendent Sizemore) and back to basics in Competency-Based Curriculum (Superintendent Reed). The USOE moved from a laissez-faire attitude of support for decentralization in Anacostia to a more hard-nosed emphasis on project activities and accomplishments. The NIE entered its negotiations with the Anacostia projects (now called RENP) with the goal of producing goal-oriented, valid educational lessons.

The Lessons of the Anacostia Experience

Our finding that the Anacostia projects fail to confirm the descriptive accuracy of the conventional implementation model is not a new one. Indeed, most recent students of implementation have found that policymaking and policy implementation can occur simultaneously.[5] Our first conclusion about Anacostia merely confirms those findings: time, resource, and information constraints lead policymakers to initiate vague policies that implementers are expected to define. In this section, we are primarily interested in the implications of such findings for people interested in improving policy implementation.

The Anacostia experience is unusual in the length of time involved (a full decade) in defining and implementing policy. Agreement on a single policy and its implementation was achieved by the NIE and RENP only in the final years of the project. During the decade, about $10 million was expended on the project.

Despite these difficulties, some things were accomplished. Even without a policy consensus, many community goals were achieved by the increase in local participation. Yet federal policymakers' initial goal of the development and implementation of a single educational policy through federal-community cooperation was not accomplished until the very end of the projects' existence. Agreement on policy early in the projects' history would have been important, because it would have increased coordination and efficiency in the use of resources; additionally, the technical lessons of such a clear policy could have been used to help other urban school districts. In this narrow but important sense, the Anacostia experience was a failure, because policy was not produced and implemented in a timely fashion. Learning the lessons that lie behind these delays, then, will be the basis of our contribution to the study of policy implementation.

Our work on Anacostia, and the work of other researchers, pointed out the difficulties associated with defining a policy once a program is in operation. This has led some researchers to argue that policymakers should definitively state policies prior to implementation, converting the empirical claims of the conventional model into a normative imperative (Lowi, 1969). Others have pointed out that policymakers who deal with complex and emotional issues lack the information and degree of goal consensus necessary for such policy pronouncements (Schlesinger, 1968). We will confine our attention to examining how policies could have been defined after policymakers decided to commit resources to future programs.

Once President Johnson made his initial commitment to an experimental school project in the District of Columbia, it was up to federal, local, and community authorities to define the policy to be pursued by that project. We believe there are three basic scenarios whereby participants could have agreed on a single policy and could have been expected to implement that policy. These scenarios are plausible extrapolations from the facts, each leading to an agreement on a policy by a different route. By comparing each scenario with actual events, we get a better appreciation of special difficulties associated with achieving policy agreements through each route. The scenarios are: agreement through mutual adjustment, through bargaining, and through the use of political power.[6]

The Mutual-Adjustment Scenario

In this instance, participants arrive at a common policy through a process of mutual adjustment based on commonly held goals. Game theorists call this a simple coordination game in which each participant voluntarily alters his behavior to achieve a common goal (Schelling, 1963). Social psychologists refer to these same relationships as *referent* power relationships (French and Raven, 1960). In the literature on educational change, McLaughlin's (1976) discussion of mutual adaptation is a good example of a policy arrived at in this fashion. The definition of policy in the mutual-adjustment scenario is merely a formalization of a preexisting consensus among participants. This scenario offers a number of advantages; it is voluntary, requires little coercion, and participants share a common incentive to cooperate and live up to their obligations.

Although many interviewees talked as if the mutual-adjustment scenario should have applied to Anacostia (for example, "we are all interested in the children"), the requirements of that scenario were simply too high to make it appropriate as a means of achieving agreement on a plan. The mutual-adjustment scenario requires a high degree of certainty about the means of achieving those goals. Our case materials indicate that although some goals were shared, there was no agreement on the relative priorities of educational, organizational, or political goals.

In addition, agreement on goals only translates to agreement on means when the technology for achieving goals is clear. The technology for achieving the shared goals of improved education was far from certain and was itself an item of dispute (community involvement versus inservice training, and so on).

Under different circumstances, goal agreement might have been achieved by the simple expedient of limiting participation to those who agreed, but the initial White House-USOE-DCPS decision to involve the community precluded such an approach. Or agreement on means could have been achieved by stating goals for which "means" were already known, as in nutrition and health programs, but the decision to develop new approaches to urban education precluded narrow goals and/or certain means.

The Bargaining Scenario

Here participants recognize they have common and divergent goals, and seek the policy most favorable to them through bargaining. A bargain is struck, or a policy made, when each side has achieved as much as it believes possible. The policy in this scenario represents a series of obligations binding on both parties and usually includes specific incentives for compliance and disincentives for noncompliance.

The bargaining scenario is often thought of as more sophisticated or realistic than mutual adjustment for gaining policy agreement. The NIE, for example, tried to use its control over RENP's continued funding as a bargaining instrument to get RENP to formulate and agree on a policy that could be implemented and would produce educational results. The NIE recognized that RENP had some divergent goals stemming from its definition of community control, but the bargaining strategy was intended to bring these goals into line with an agreement on an overall policy.

A number of factors together worked against the success of the bargaining scenario in Anacostia. At minimum, the bargaining strategy requires bargainers who are empowered to deal on behalf of their side and are capable of complying with the policy agreed on. Anacostia's representatives in NIE-RENP negotiations often lacked such characteristics, since the community board retained the authority to dismiss project directors with whom they were displeased. The NIE tried bargaining directly with the board, but this was also difficult because the board membership was politically divided and was liable to change at periodic elections.

At other times, the NIE sought to bargain with the DCPS, the nominal recipients of federal funds for Anacostia. But the District leadership in the superintendent's office tended to be unstable because of its involvement in conflicts with the citywide Board of Education, and was often unwilling to become embroiled in what was considered an Anacostia problem.

A further problem was the inability of Anacostia participants to live up to bargained agreements once concluded. Successful bargaining, after all, requires bargainers with the capability of enforcing agreements. In some instances, the means of compliance were beyond the control of Anacostia participants, because they were dependent on others: the District of Columbia Public Schools and its cumbersome internal procedures for hiring project staff and for securing supplies; outside consultants to devise and implement new and untried staff training programs, and so on.

Finally, this scenario requires policies with realistic provisions for the enforcement of agreements. Unlike the mutual-adjustment scenario, bargaining assumes that participants will interpret policy agreements according to their separate interests. The best mechanism is to "pay on performance"; that is, provide the promised benefit of an agreement when a condition is met (Stevens, 1974).

Unfortunately, such direct incentives were not available to the NIE, which had to pay for RENP operations in advance of providing the promised services. Furthermore, the NIE, like other federal agencies, had an incentive to "move money" through commitments to projects prior to the expiration of the fiscal year, or risk losing a portion of their congressional appropriation. So, at times, the NIE could not threaten to withhold funds until an agreement was reached or compliance occurred. Instead, it had to promise funds to the project and then bargain over their use, thereby reducing the effectiveness of their most powerful incentive, a financial one. The NIE sought to increase the frequency and specificity of negotiations in an attempt to work around these bargaining limitations.

Like the mutual-adjustment scenario, the bargaining scenario might have worked better under different circumstances. Had RENP been a more monolithic actor, with greater control over compliance, then the bargaining scenario would have been more appropriate. Something like this did occur with RENP, as the director gained more power and as the composition of the board shifted, but these developments took an inordinately long time. It is, after all, an extremely cumbersome bargaining scenario that requires the creation of effective bargaining agents before the process can effectively begin.

The Political-Power Scenario

Political theorists agree that fundamental societal conflicts over values are resolved through the exercise of power. The use of power is appropriate when other means of deciding conflicts are unavailable. A policy definition and implementation scenario that follows from this view is that one party simply imposes its policy preferences on the other, and the other has no choice but to comply. In such a scenario, federal educational authorities would have listed their requirements for a policy, and Anacostia then would have had to decide whether to develop a policy within the required framework in order to get federal funds.

Stated in such a raw form, the political-power scenario seems unattractive because it conflicts with other values. In the Anacostia case, such a position is inconsistent with the values of local autonomy, with the vision of a cooperative federal-local partnership, and with federal agencies' conceptions of themselves.

Despite these and other misgivings, the prospect that power could be used as a substitute for final voluntary agreement remains an open one. Such power need not be exercised at the outset of negotiations. It might be applied when agreement is close but the final steps continue to elude negotiators.

This scenario was not available because federal agencies did not have the option of using power authoritatively. In 1972, the USOE's efforts to cut off support was reversed by the projects' supporters in the White House and Congress. Similarly, the NIE's use of the threat of termination was constrained by congressional "earmarking" of appropriations for Anacostia and the threat of more vigorous outside intervention. It was only after the prospects for such outside intervention waned, in the final years of the experiment, that the NIE could plausibly threaten to use power to settle disputes.

Of course, one might simply reverse the political-power scenario and look at the prospects for Anacostia imposing their preferences on federal agencies. The problem remained, since the Anacostia project participants lacked authoritative power over the agencies. Although Anacostia could call on powerful outside allies, these outsiders did not and would not impose Anacostia's overall policy preferences on those agencies.

The prospect of outside intervention, then, prevented federal agencies from using the authority or power necessary to impose agreements. As time passed, the likelihood of intervention diminished—owing to changes in Anacostia and in the political environment of Capitol Hill—and the ability of the NIE to use the threat of power increased. Over time, RENP became more compliant as the strength of the NIE's position increased. But again, these changes occurred only after a decade of effort, and so cannot be considered a success.

Summary

We have described the history of the Anacostia projects, some conclusions based on that history, and some lessons for other federal efforts to plan and implement policy through the use of community intermediaries. We have explored three alternative scenarios for gaining agreement on policy and for increasing the likelihood of faithful implementation. For each scenario, we have described why the Anacostia experience failed to fulfill the necessary requirements. It is clear that these failings are not because of the faults of individual participants—each of whom pursued plausible, realistic, and even laudable goals—but rather, are because of structural shortcomings beyond the control of individual actors.

Notes

1. Interviews were conducted during two time periods: Dianne Pinderhughes studied the aspects of community control during 1970-1971, and she and

Robert Nakamura investigated the more general context of the projects during 1976–1977. Our interviewees included people from the following organizations: the Johnson White House staff, the United States Office of Education, the National Institutes of Education, the District of Columbia Public Schools, the staff and boards of the Anacostia projects, education groups within the District, and from the *Washington Post.* In many instances, these interviews were supplemented by the files of many of the organizations named. See Robert Nakamura and Dianne Pinderhughes, "A History of Federal Educational Projects in Anacostia" (Report to Gibboney Associates); and Dianne Pinderhughes, "Politics and Decentralization in Washington, D.C.: "The Anacostia Community School Project" (Master's thesis, University of Chicago, 1971).

2. For a more general statement of this problem, see Mancur Olson, "Evaluating Performance in the Public Sector," in *The Measurement of Economic and Social Performance,* ed. Milton Moss (New York: National Bureau of Economic Research, 1975).

3. This conventional model derives from several intellectual traditions: Woodrow Wilson's influential distinction between politics and administration separating the policymaking function of elected officials from the administrative responsibilities of bureaucrats; Max Weber's teachings about the technical superiority of bureaucracy as an instrument for the achievement of governmental goals; and the formalization of these and other views into the classical conception of public administration. For a discussion of the assumptions, see Robert Nakamura and Frank Smallwood, *The Politics of Policy Implementation* (New York: St. Martin's, 1980), chap. 2. Such a view can often be found, among other places, in the assumptions of the Requests for Proposals (RFPs) used by federal education agencies to solicit contractors.

4. From 1967 to 1977, the District of Columbia Public Schools had six superintendents or acting superintendents; the Anacostia projects had seven project directors or acting directors, and numerous different elected board members.

5. Specific case studies making this point include: Radin, *Implementation, Change;* Jerome Murphy, "Title I of ESEA: The Politics of Implementing Federal Education Reform," *Harvard Educational Review* 41, no. 1 (1971); Jerome Murphy, "The Education Bureaucracies Implement Novel Policy: The Politics of Title I of ESEA, 1965-72," in *Policy and Politics in America,* ed. Allan P. Sindler (Boston: Little, Brown, 1977); Daniel P. Moynihan, *Maximum Feasible Misunderstanding* (New York: Free Press, 1970); Bernard Frieden and Marshall Kaplan, *The Politics of Neglect* (Cambridge, Mass.: MIT Press, 1975). For more general discussions of the process of defining policy during implementation, see Rein and Rabinowitz, "Theoretical Perspective"; Bardach, *Implementation Game;* Michael Lipsky, "Standing the Study of Implementation on Its Head," in *Politics and Policy: The United States in the 1970s,* ed. W.D. Burnham and M.W. Weinberg (Cambridge, Mass.: MIT Press, 1979); Nakamura and Smallwood, *Politics of Policy,* chapter 3.

6. For a further discussion of such scenarios, see Robert Nakamura, "Strategies for Defining Policy Implementation," in *Proceedings of the Research Conference on Public Policy Management,* ed. John P. Crecine (forthcoming).

References

Bardach, Eugene. *The Implementation Game.* Cambridge, Mass.: MIT Press, 1977.

Cooper, Bruce S. "Beyond Implementation." *ERIC,* 1978.

French, John R.P., Jr., and Raven, Bertram. "The Bases of Social Power." In *Group Dynamics,* edited by Dorwin Cartwright and Alvin Zander, pp. 608-610. Evanston, Ill.: Row, Peterson, and Co., 1960.

Lindblom, Charles E. "The Science of Muddling Through." *Public Administration Review* 19 (Spring 1979): 79-88.

Lowi, Theodore. *The End of Liberalism.* New York: Norton, 1969.

McLaughlin, Milbrey. "Implementation as Mutual Adaptation." In *Social Program Implementation,* edited by Walter Williams and Richard Elmore. San Francisco: Academic Press, 1976.

Pressman, Jeffrey L., and Wildavsky, Aaron. *Implementation.* Berkeley: University of California Press, 1973.

Radin, Beryl. *Implementation, Change and the Federal Bureaucracy.* New York: Columbia University Press, 1978.

Rein, Martin, and Rabinowitz, Francine. "Implementation: A Theoretical Perspective." In *American Politics and Public Policy,* edited by W.D. Burnham and M.W. Weinberg. Cambridge, Mass.: MIT Press, 1978.

Schelling, Thomas. *The Strategy of Conflict.* pp. 3-4, 5-6, 16-19. New York: Oxford University Press, 1963.

Schlesinger, James. "Systems Analysis and the Political Process" *Journal of Law and Economics* 11 (October 1968): 281-289.

Stevens, Robert, and Stevens, Rosemary. *Welfare Medicine in America.* New York: The Free Press of Macmillan, 1974.

Sullivan, Denis; Nakamura, Robert; and Winters, Richard. "Political Reform and Control of Administration." In *How America Is Ruled,* chapter 16. New York: John Wiley, 1980.

Wildavsky, Aaron B. "The Political Economy of Efficiency: Cost-Benefit Analysis, Systems Analysis, and Program Budgeting." *Public Administration Review* (December 1966): 292-310.

2

Policy Drift: An Evaluation of the California Business Enterprise Program

Guenther Kress, Gustav Koehler, and J. Fred Springer

We were drifting. We were like a boat going down the river without a motor, but we were still in relatively gentle waters—we hadn't gone over the waterfall. At this point, we asked for an evaluation of the Business Enterprise Program.

Roger Krum, Administrator
The California Business Enterprise Program

Typically, the day-to-day process of implementing a program involves a series of focused decisions in response to rather specific, and frequently unconnected, problems. Initially, most of these decisions do not seem momentous in their consequences, they represent more or less reasonable accommodations within the overall program order set by the enabling legislation and regulations. However, as time goes by, the consequences of these decisions may cumulatively bring changes that fundamentally alter the program and its objectives.

This alteration of program and policy is probably inevitable, and may be desirable, as program managers and street-level bureaucrats seek to creatively and responsively implement programs in unique environments. However, if decision makers lose sight of the reasons for changes that have occurred in program activities and objectives, and if they do not understand the resulting cumulative effect of these changes, confusion and conflict within the program can build. Program managers, legislators, political executives, and important client or interest groups, may disagree over priorities and objectives, performance standards, strategies, and ultimately the nature of the program itself.

Under these circumstances, the essentially creative process of policy implementation can begin to lose direction. Without a clear understanding of the genesis and motivation of competing demands within and without the program, decision makers may react to conflicts without criteria to resolve them, and the program will *drift* in response to this buffeting.

The authors contend that evaluators can help remedy *policy drift* by identifying the reasons for competing demands on a program and by clarifying changes that have occurred in program activities and objectives. Indeed, the evaluator may be alerted to the necessity of this role when program confusion prevents the ready identification of evaluative standards. The remainder of this chapter develops a preliminary model of the process of policy drift in the hopes of providing a starting point for evaluators attempting to analyze the process.

Grounding the Concept of Policy Drift

Since the understanding of policy drift must be grounded in the actual behavior and decisions of policymakers and program managers, we have chosen to develop our initial clarification of drift through the evaluation of an existing program—the Business Enterprise Program (BEP) of the California Department of Rehabilitation.

The Business Enterprise Program is a unique, federally sponsored, state-administrated program that places rehabilitated blind persons as vendors in food-service facilities such as vending stands, snack bars, and cafeterias that are established and supported by the program. Vendors derive their income from the profits of their location. In the 34 years since the initial implementation in California, the BEP has grown into a statewide business that grosses $23 million in annual sales, nets more than $4 million in income to more than 300 blind vendors, and provides employment for approximately 750 other people, many of them handicapped. By many standards, including long-term growth, and satisfaction of both vendors and service contractees, the program is highly successful.

Nevertheless, the California Department of Rehabilitation perceived the need for a comprehensive evaluation of program objectives, performance, and future options. The reasons behind the department's request were directly related to the phenomenon of policy drift. Over the years, the operations of the BEP were increasingly a subject of disagreement and confusion. Key department decision makers perceived the BEP as diverging from the department's major purposes in vocational rehabilitation, and the department's interest in integrating disabled persons into the mainstream of society. Program clients and other participants disagreed with many of the department's emerging demands and placed program management under competing pressures. The evaluation was largely a product of this perceived need to clarify the role of the BEP within the department's larger policy objectives.

In addition to this original impetus for evaluation, other factors recommend the BEP as a case study in policy drift. The program has a long history of implementation—original authorization at the federal level came through the Randolph-Sheppard Act of 1936, and the California legislature authorized the state's program in 1945. This long history and the state-level implementation of a federally mandated program offer a promising opportunity to observe the processes and consequences of drift.

Figure 2-1 shows the process of drift in California's Business Enterprise Program. The categories therein do not exhaust the process and consequences

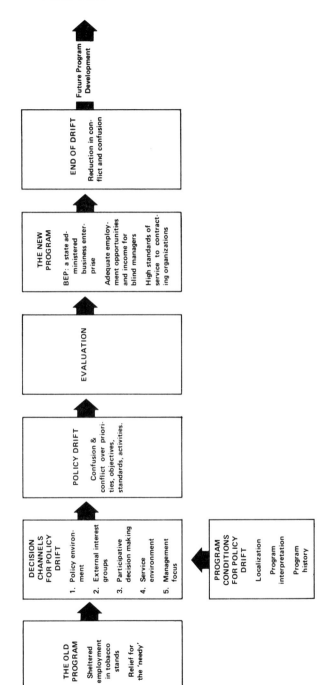

Figure 2-1. The Process of Policy Drift Origins, Manifestations, and Consequences

that may accompany drift; their refinement depends on application to other programs and policy environments. However, the figure does provide a first model of drift that is grounded in one case study. It synopsizes the original order of the BEP as mandated in the Randolph-Sheppard Act. The rationale for that legislation was clearly stated in the report of the Senate Committee on Education and Labor:

> The Federal Government is spending billions of dollars to create employment opportunities for millions of persons, but not one blind person is benefitted thereby. The blind cannot build bridges, buildings, and do other kinds of work now being authorized by the Public Works Administration.[1]

Thus, for the purposes of "providing blind persons with remunerative employment," and "enlarging the economic opportunities of the blind,"[2] the act authorized blind persons to operate vending stands in federal buildings, such as post offices. It is important to note that the original legislation authorized a program that:

1. Provided appropriate employment for blind persons in the form of small tobacco and dry-goods stands in building lobbies
2. Was aimed at the needy blind who were not getting relief from other programs
3. Allowed the use of federal buildings to house vending stands at the discretion of building managers
4. Provided minimal support for vendors once the location was made available

Thus, the original legislation represented a token effort to help the blind defray economic hardship by providing them with sheltered employment opportunities appropriate to their disability. Blindness was seen as a major obstacle to participation in the competitive labor market.

In the thirty-five years since California's program was established, the BEP has been slowly transformed. Many of the changes passed virtually unnoticed until the late 1970s when events brought conflicts to a head. Figure 2-1 identifies some of the program conditions and decision channels that contributed to drift in the BEP. Since the conditions for drift, the decision channels through which it occurs, and its consequences are the central components of the model, each of these areas will be considered in more detail

Program Conditions for Drift

A condition that first contributed to drift in the BEP was the need for *localization.* Policies that are devised for large geographic areas must be made specific for local environments. The Randolph-Sheppard Act authorized federal sponsorship and matched funding for state-level programs to employ blind vendors.

These programs required additional state-level authorization, which may carry mandates that modify federal intent. The California legislature, for instance, has placed limits on the portion of a vendor's income that may be set aside for additional program purposes. This state requirement affects the ability of California's program managers to implement some other permissible policies in the federal mandate—such as income redistribution to vendors who are "stuck" in locations that have poor business potential.

A second area in which drift may occur can be referred to as *program interpretation*. At the most formal level, one could see this type of drift as the discrepancies between legislation and administrative regulations, but the importance of program interpretation extends well beyond the writing of regulations. Management decisions on budget requests, job descriptions, and other standard administrative functions subtly shape the direction of the program. Program mandates differ greatly in the degree to which the administrative and organizational means for implementing the program are specified. As the discretion for program interpretation grows, so does the potential for drift.

Third, policy drift is likely to be at least partly a function of the length and nature of the program's *history*. Long-standing programs that have operated under conditions requiring significant adaptation have potential for drift. This potential may be increased if the program has not come under frequent scrutiny in the past.

The potential for drift in the BEP is clear: (1) the program is federally sponsored and locally implemented through a state agency; (2) the program is unique (that is, a state-administered business venture)—and the means for implementation are not specified legislatively, nor are they clearly articulated in the "umbrella" Department of Rehabilitation; and (3) the program in California is thirty-five years old.

Decision Channels for Policy Drift

The development of a model of policy drift to guide the evaluator must go beyond the identification of conditions that enhance the prospects of drift. An adequate model must identify how and why decisions are made that carry consequences for program objectives. In our evaluation of the California BEP, we identified five major channels for policy or implementation decisions that contributed to drift (see figure 2-1). A brief discussion of each channel will clarify the consequences of drift for the BEP.

Policy Environment

Public programs do not operate in isolation, particularly in an intergovernmental system with overlapping jurisdictions and fragmented functional mandates. Complementary or competing programs may begin, end, or be modified—changing the needs or expectations in a given policy area.

Federal legislation requires that agencies administering the program be housed in the state-level departments for vocational rehabilitation. During the late 1960s and early 1970s, the dominant policy perspective in vocational rehabilitation came under serious scrutiny and challenge. There was movement away from a narrow focus on employability as a rehabilitation objective toward a broader concern with the whole person, a movement from professionalized counseling and support to self-help and mainstreaming in society, and an emphasis on the individual rights of disabled persons. These new emphases in rehabilitation philosophy were reflected in the federal Rehabilitation Act of 1973 and received particular attention in California with the appointment of a department director with strong ties to the new independent-living perspective.

Thus, the policy environment around the BEP changed dramatically during the early 1970s. One consequence of this change was the growing misunderstanding and suspicion of the program among department policymakers who came to perceive the BEP as an inefficient and anachronistic mechanism for rehabilitation. From their perspective, the BEP appeared to rehabilitate very few disabled persons and to isolate and shelter vendors from the competitive labor market—thereby discouraging independence and self-help. This drift between the objectives of the BEP and the department did not occur because of program decisions during implementation, but because of legislative and higher-level administrative changes in policy. Nevertheless, the growing discrepancy between department objectives and the perceived objectives of the BEP was sufficient to prompt a comprehensive evaluation of the program.

External Interest Groups

The blind community in America has long been a well organized and effective champion of public programs for blind persons. As a result of pressure from interest groups for the blind, the Randolph-Sheppard Act has been amended twice, in 1954 and 1974. California legislation has been subject to more than a dozen legislative amendments. Congress and the California legislature shifted the BEP's mandate away from creating more opportunities for blind entrepreneurs toward supporting and protecting the income and advancement of vendors in the program. This shift has contributed to conflict and confusion over the roles of vendors and program staff. It became unclear whether vendors were clients of a rehabilitation program, franchise managers, or independent business persons. The results were conflicting expectations and increasing tension between vendors and the BEP staff.

Participative Decision Making

As part of the 1974 amendments, the federal government mandated that vendor's policy committees participate with the state agency "in major administrative decisions and policy and program development." In California, program vendors elect representatives to the California Vendor's Policy Committee (CVPC) which meets regularly to request information from program management, deliberate on program policy issues, and make recommendations. Although the CVPC certainly exerts pressures for management decisions that affect program objectives, the nature of this influence is complicated by at least two factors.

First, the legislated mandate for participation does not specify the authority of the CVPC. Although it is implied that its role is more than advisory, the intended nature of its contribution to decisions is vague. Second, the CVPC's claim to representativeness is somewhat tenuous. Many vendors are isolated from other colleagues. Indeed, only 12 percent of a random sample of vendors felt that the CVPC represented vendors' interests "very well," and one-third did not feel informed enough about CVPC activities to express an opinion. In sum, the selection and participation of CVPC members are not necessarily representative of the broad interests of all vendors in the program, and this possibility complicates the committee's role in program decisions.

One consequence of this confusion over the CVPC role has been a style of participation in which the CVPC has tended to champion rather specific vendors' interests vis-à-vis program management. This orientation contributes to conflict between vendors and program staff who are seen as targets for increased demands, and has fueled concerns in the Department of Rehabilitation that the BEP disproportionately benefits a rather small number of disabled persons.

Service Environment

Another source of drift in the BEP came from the changing environment in which the program provided services. In the early years of the Randolph-Sheppard programs, vendors were restricted to small tobacco-stand locations that offered a limited variety of items for purchase. As government grew and employees became more oriented toward eating meals away from home, the need and opportunity for a much greater variety of food-service facilities beckoned. Today, the California BEP places vendors in a variety of locations from small dry-vending standards to large, full-service cafeterias, many of which gross over half a million dollars in annual sales.

The program's responsiveness to changes in the service environment has necessitated modification in operating objectives. The provision of food services to employees, for example, is an important functional concern for managers of public buildings. Accepting this service role has meant that the BEP must place a higher priority on maintaining effective communications with contractees and on insuring some means of service quality control. One result is tension between management and vendors over the program's ability to require certain standards of performance and to impose sanctions when they are not met.

Management Focus

A final source of pressures for drift in the BEP was associated with an inward focus on daily management decisions. Indeed, in group interviews, program managers agreed that the maintenance of existing locations and the use of management resources to enhance their income potential were the highest-priority operating objectives in the program. These priorities certainly were not clearly anticipated in the modest expectations of the original Randolph-Sheppard legislation.

Although many of such pressures have contributed to this ordering of program priorities, there are internal considerations that reinforce it. For example, in the area of personnel administration, program staff are assigned to oversee the vendors on a case-worker model. Each business enterprise officer has a generalized responsibility to evaluate and provide support for a given number of vendors. This personnel decision had the consequence of pushing program operations toward a one-to-one counseling orientation to vendors. It tended to focus management attention on keeping vendors happy and detracted from the functional need for a system of food-service outlets (for example, market research, promotion strategy, state-of-the-art training).

In sum, the cumulative impact of drift in these channels was sufficient to create a crisis in program identity by the mid-1970s. The California Department of Finance foresaw this crisis in a 1975 report on the BEP. They observed that the program's most basic difficulties stemmed from a:

> conflict of primary purpose: should the program provide "opportunity and rehabilitation for the blind" with service to customers as a necessary, but secondary purpose, or should the program be a "business" program which provides service to consumers, and, secondarily, opportunity and rehabilitation for the blind.[3]

Still, the clarification and positive resolution of this confusion awaited a full evaluation of the BEP in 1979.

Remedying Drift in the BEP

Disagreement over whether BEP is a rehabilitation program or a business program led to confusion about its place in the department, confusion regarding the functions of BEP's and other staff members, and confusion among vendors concerning their role in the program. Most important, the lack of a clear and shared statement of program objectives contributed to a highly politicized decision-making environment that retarded the resolution of crucial policy issues. The competing images of the BEP implied different means of accomplishing objectives and contributed to vacillation and stagnation. Early in the evaluation, it became clear that the study would have to proceed in a way that articulated the nature and causes of competing program images, rather than relying on the measurement of program results against previously defined standards.

A detailed discussion of evaluative techniques goes beyond the limits of this chapter. Indeed, the evaluation of the BEP relied on many standard tools, such as flow charting, content analysis of legislation and regulations, a staff workload study, cost-benefit analysis, and on-site depth interviews with a hundred vendors. Group interviews with major program participants (such as program managers, the CVPC) took on special importance because of their utility in clarifying disagreement and confusions.

The evaluators developed a structured group interview format that fit the evaluative needs of a program experiencing drift. This format guided interviewees in a process that:

1. Identified major groups making demands on the program
2. Prioritized groups according to the perceived importance of their demands
3. Identified specific objectives of each group
4. Prioritized group objectives
5. Identified conflicts between objectives
6. Identified opportunities and constraints for meeting objectives and resolving conflict
7. Assessed the opportunities and constraints in terms of seriousness and urgency.

This exercise contributed significantly to understanding policy drift as it occurred in the BEP.[4]

The major accomplishment of the evaluation was the clarification of the nature of the BEP. The evaluators concluded that the BEP must be characterized as a state-administered business enterprise. The BEP is not a rehabilitation program with services comparable to those provided through the Department of Rehabilitation's vocational rehabilitation programs. Rehabilitation is a process through which a disabled person is provided assistance in preparing to compete for employment opportunities. As a business enterprise, the BEP is not intended to prepare blind persons for opportunities; it is intended to provide opportunities for business enterprise. Nor is the BEP a sheltered workshop where individuals are employees rather than managers. Finally, the BEP is not a loose collection of publicly subsidized, independent businesses that are controlled by individual proprietors. The BEP is a single enterprise that operates a large number of vending facilities throughout the state, and therefore has unique responsibilities to customers, contracting organizations, and vendors.

Notes

1. U.S. Cong., *Report to Accompany H.R. 4688.*
2. 20 U.S. Code 107 (1).
3. Calif. Dept. Finance, *Business Enterprise,* p. 47.
4. More detailed information regarding this tool can be obtained from California Technical Assistance Associates, Inc., 2015 21st Street, Sacramento, Calif. 95818.

References

California Department of Finance. *Business Enterprise Program.* Sacramento, Calif.: Department of Finance, December 1975, p. 47.
U.S. Congress, Senate, Committee on Education and Labor. *Report to Accompany H.R. 4688.* 74th Cong., 2nd sess., S. Rept. 2052, May 12, 1936, p. 2.

3 Organizational Goals and Their Impact on the Policy Implementation Process

George E. Rawson

The models of the policy implementation process that have been posited over the last few years frequently cite organizational goals as an important independent variable in explaining the level of implementation success (Van Meter and Van Horn, 1975; Sabatier and Mazmanian, 1979). Most research asserts that successful implementation requires a clearly stated organizational goal that is subscribed to by the organization's leaders. Sabatier and Mazmanian (1979), for example, write that one requirement for successful implementation is that "the Statute [or other basic policy decision] contains unambiguous policy directives . . . [and that] the leaders of the implementing agencies . . . are committed to statutory goals."

Such models are, by definition, oversimplifcations of reality. In reality, the relationship between organizational goals and the implementation process is far more complex. If policy analysts are to contribute to the optimizing of public policies, it is essential that relationships such as this one be scrutinized in great detail. By examining the relationship between goals and implementation success and failure, we will get a better understanding of the conditions necessary for successful implementation.

As a step toward this understanding, this chapter presents a case study of the Tennessee Valley Authority (TVA) as one instance of successful implementation.[1] The relationship between goals and implementation is particularly important in this case, because the TVA not only has supplemented an initially nebulous statement of goals, but also has succeeded in implementing decisions aimed at achieving those goals. Although the TVA has several programs, because of space limitations this chapter will focus on its principal program of power.[2]

Background

The problems that eventually resulted in the establishment of the TVA were originally transportation and navigation on the Tennessee River. In particular, a 37-mile stretch of the river near Muscle Shoals, Alabama was virtually impassable

The author is indebted to Richard Campbell of the University of Georgia and Susan Kay and Douglas Shumavon of Miami University for helpful comments and suggestions.

because of a 134-foot drop in the river. The federal government expressed concern about these problems as early as 1824. Efforts to bring the river under control, however, found little support in Congress.

It was not until American involvement in World War I seemed imminent that Congress finally acted. As part of the "preparedness legislation of 1916," Congress authorized construction of a nitrate plant and dam at Muscle Shoals (McGraw, 1971). Nitrate, at the time, was an important ingredient in munitions. The main purpose of the dam was to provide electricity for the nitrate plant. Nitrate, however, was also a principal ingredient for fertilizer. Since the states around Alabama were in need of such fertilizer, Muscle Shoals was a logical site for the plant (Owen, 1973). Thus, after the war, when the munitions were no longer needed, the nitrate could be used to produce fertilizer.

Debate in Congress over what to do with the partially completed nitrate plant and dam began immediately after the war. However, it was not until 1933 and the inauguration of President Roosevelt that legislation was passed establishing the TVA and giving it control over the dormant plant and dam.

The TVA Act

The preamble to the TVA's enabling legislation does not mention electricity generation or distribution, but less than fifty years later the TVA has become the nation's largest consumer of coal, and is constructing the nation's largest nuclear power plant. The TVA's activity as an electric utility has become so massive that it dwarfs the agency's other programs and consumed 95.3 percent of its total expenditures in fiscal year 1978 (*Tennessee Valley Authority Annual Report*, 1978).

Congress, in creating the TVA, realized electricity would play some role in improving the quality of life in the Tennessee Valley, but it was certainly perceived as playing much less of a role than it actually does today. Although electricity generation is mentioned in several places in the TVA Act, it is qualified in two important ways. First, Congress asserted that state, county, and local governments, as well as domestic consumers be given priority over industrial users (TVA Act, 1933). Further, when electricity generation is mentioned in the act, it is clearly distinguished as something that will occur incidental to the more primary purposes of the agency. In section 23 of the Act, for example, electricity generation is clearly intended as subordinate to "flood control and navigation." It should also be noted that despite the technological feasibility of coal, oil, and natural-gas plants in 1933, nowhere in the act is there mention of the TVA using nonhydro means of generating electricity, all of which are in use today in addition to nuclear and pumped-water storage.[3]

The Early Years: 1933–1939

During this time period, TVA officials, and especially the three-member board of directors, laid important groundwork that would serve as the building block for future development of the agency and its goals. The wide-ranging responsibilities charged to the boards in the enabling legislation provided little direction for establishing new programs. Consulting with President Roosevelt provided little help as the members were told essentially to "go to it" (McGraw, 1970). The board members were thus left with the rare opportunity of establishing both an organization and its goals with "no traditions to guide them and no precedents to follow" (Owen, 1973).

The first goal to emerge in agency writings was "unified resource development." The first annual report, covering 1934, noted "surveys and studies are under way leading to a single unified plan for the development of the entire Tennessee River system for navigation, flood control, and power development" (*Annual Report,* 1935, p. 4). However, this nebulous statement left agency leaders free to attempt to force their own interpretations on the agency. Indeed, conflict among board members and between the agency and its environment over how to best achieve this nebulous goal was a prominent aspect of the agency's early history.

Soon after the board began work, conflict erupted between Arthur Morgan, the board's first chairman, and one of the other members, David E. Lilienthal. The board had informally agreed that each member should be given control over certain agency programs. But Arthur Morgan, whose realm was engineering and construction, had a different view of the agency's purpose than did Lilienthal, who was responsible for the power program.[4] Although both subscribed to the goal of unified resource development, Lilienthal believed this should be done in such a way as to improve the plight of the Valley's residents. Arthur Morgan, however, viewed the agency as a social experiment, the results of which could be applied to other parts of the nation.[5]

Given his desire to improve human conditions in the Valley as rapidly as possible, combined with his view of private power companies as only profit oriented, Lilienthal moved to construct a power program exclusive of the private power companies operating in the Valley. Arthur Morgan, on the other hand, desired cooperation with the private power companies and opposed Lilienthal at every opportunity, and went so far as to actively oppose Lilienthal's renomination to the board in 1936. The feud did not end until Roosevelt intervened in 1938 and removed Arthur Morgan from the board. In the meantime, Harcourt Morgan, after trying to remain neutral, sided with Lilienthal. The resultant majority votes allowed Lilienthal to work to exclude private power companies from operating in the Valley.

Even more volatile than the feud between Morgan and Lilienthal was the ongoing conflict between the TVA and its environment. Dozens of law suits were filed by private power companies attempting to preserve their bailiwicks and stop the TVA from becoming a power distributor. The issue was not settled until 1939 when the Supreme Court ruled that the private power companies lacked proper standing to sue (*Tennessee Electric*, 1939). Although the decision did not address the central question of TVA's legal authority to operate a full-scale power program, it effectively prevented the private power companies from bringing any further lawsuits on this matter. Thus, by 1939, the feud within the TVA had been settled, the major environmental opponent had been denied its principal weapon, and the already well-entrenched power program had been established as a principal implementation tool to achieve the agency's goal of unified resource development.[6]

The War and Postwar Years

World War II was a period of peaceful growth at the TVA. Because nationwide attention was focused on the war, generating capacity grew to five times the size it had been in 1939. The agency was so successful in establishing its service area that in 1943, C. Herman Pritchett wrote:

> The T.V.A. had thus . . . carried through a program of negotiation and purchase which put practically every city in Tennessee, as well as in many adjacent states, in the power business. In all, 83 municipalities were contracting for T.V.A. power by July, 1942.

More important than simple expansion, however, was an instrumental change to a coal-fired generating plant that had been constructed to meet wartime demand for electricity. Although the legality of such a move was obviously questionable, it went unchallenged because of wartime need. However, in the postwar years, opposition to such plants from private power companies was the dominant activity in the agency's environment.

After the war, when demand for electricity in the Valley began to exceed hydroelectric capacity, the abundant coal in the area was a logical source for a new generator fuel. When the TVA requested funds from Congress to construct a coal-fired steam plant in its fiscal year 1949 budget, the issue was much broader than funds for a single plant. Until this time, electricity generation, theoretically, had been incidental to flood control or necessary for the war effort. Now, however, the agency wanted to construct a plant for the sole purpose of meeting an increase in the demand for electricity that, in large part, the TVA had caused.[7] If Congress appropriated the necessary funds, it would be legitimizing the TVA's role as a power utility.

During the appropriation hearings, several private power companies expressed vehement opposition to the TVA's construction of coal-fired steam plants. This opposition was especially strong from those companies whose service areas bordered the TVA's. They feared the TVA would overbuild and use its excess capacity as an excuse to expand its service area. Despite support from President Truman, Congress refused to appropriate the funds in 1948. Only after Truman's surprise reelection and a return to Democratic control of the House of Representatives did the measure pass.[8] Despite this legitimation of the TVA's power program, the private power companies continued to oppose the construction of individual coal-fired steam plants as unnecessary, and thus slowed down the authorization process and thereby plant construction. The TVA responded by requesting the power program be made self-financing through bond sales. Again, private power companies were the main opponent, fearing the TVA would use the funds acquired through bond sales to overbuild and expand their service area.

The debate raged from 1955 until 1959 when a compromise was reached. The TVA's power program would become self-financing but the agency's service area was to be frozen at its present location. When the self-financing legislation was passed, it relieved the TVA from the burden of gaining congressional approval through the appropriation's process for construction of new power plants. More important, it removed the private power companies that were the best financed and organized of TVA's critics from its environment.

Although at the end of the 1950s the TVA was still a multiprogram organization, power was becoming its dominant program. The agency, which had limited its power construction programs to dams at the beginning of World War II, was now generating more than 70 percent of its electricity with coal-fired steam plants. The power program that many had viewed as incidental to flood control was by 1959 consuming 77 percent of agency expenditures.

The 1960s—A Period of Quiet Growth

After passage of the self-financing amendment, the TVA again entered a period of quiet growth. Between 1960 and 1965 the agency increased its generating capacity from 11.4 million kilowatts to 14.7 million kilowatts. Eighty-seven percent of the increase resulted from the construction of new coal-fired steam plants which gave new prominence to electrical energy as a tool in implementing unified resource development. As measured by expenditures, the power program had accounted for half of the TVA's activity in 1951; by the end of 1966 this figure had increased to 75 percent.

While increasing in size, the power program was also increasing in importance to TVA officials. Aubrey Wagner, who had been designated chairman of the TVA board by President Kennedy in 1962, stressed that the power program was crucial. The TVA's power program had obviously evolved to become the dominant force in "program action if not program thinking." Wagner indicated that the power program was the TVA's way of contributing to economic development, regional welfare, the nation's economy, and defense. Thus, the provision of low-cost electrical energy, by this time, had come to dominate not only "program action" but also "program thinking."

During the mid-1960s, the TVA, which by then had become the nation's largest consumer of coal, was experiencing increasing problems in using that coal. Air pollution caused by coal and other fossil fuels had become a matter of public concern. More important for the TVA, however, was the increased concern being shown for the degradation of the environment caused by strip-mining. A large portion of the coal used by the TVA was being mined by this technique. In 1965 the state legislatures in Kentucky and Tennessee, the states that provided the bulk of TVA coal, were considering regulation of strip-mining. This situation made the environment for coal suppliers and users very uncertain. This uncertainty, coupled with the large quantities of coal the agency demanded of its suppliers, had an adverse effect on the availability of coal. This was dramatized early in 1966 when the TVA let bids for large quantities of coal, and none of adequate size was received.

In this environment, the TVA let bids for massive new generating capacity be brought on line in the early 1970s. For the first time the TVA did not exclude, and indeed specifically requested, bids for nuclear plants. A few months later, when the agency accepted a $122.7 million bid by General Electric for two 1,000-megawatt nuclear-power boiling water reactors (BWR), the TVA added an important new technology to its list of implementation tools. Asserting its desire to provide electricity at the lowest possible cost, the agency indicated the nuclear plant would save approximately $8 million a year over a coal-fired steam plant (Tennessee Valley Authority, 1966).

Given the high level of conflict that such changes at the TVA had generated in the past, the resulting criticisms of the agency were surprisingly mild. The principal source of criticism was the coal industry. The industry attacked the decision on two fronts: the limited liability of utilities for nuclear accidents and the uncertainty about the cost of nuclear-generated electricity. Brice O'Brien, general counsel for the National Coal Association, appeared before the Joint Atomic Energy Committee and attacked the limited liability clause of the Price-Anderson Act. O'Brien, claiming the legislation indicated the utilities' lack of faith in the safety of nuclear power, used this conclusion to criticize the TVA's potential move to nuclear power (*Knoxville News-Sentinel,* 1966). Joseph E. Moody, president of the National Coal Policy Conference Incorporated, wrote an open letter to TVA officials in which he labeled "grossly unfair" the agency's "attempt to equate an assured cost based on the utilization of coal with the speculative and conjectural costs which the utilization of nuclear power of necessity entails" (*Memphis Commercial Appeal,* 1966).

After the initial outburst of criticism by the coal industry, the TVA's environment returned to a passive state and remained that way for the rest of the 1960s. The power program continued to grow, however, with three additional nuclear units and a large coal-fired steam plant being put under construction. Total generating capacity, which had been 11,373,460 kilowatts in 1960, increased to 17,090,565 kilowatts by 1969.

Conflict Renewed—The 1970s

The calm that prevailed in the TVA's environment in the 1960s was in sharp contrast to the furor that marked that same environment in the 1970s. In an attempt to meet the seemingly ever-increasing demand for electricity in the Valley, the TVA ordered twelve more nuclear units, in addition to those ordered in the late 1960s, to be constructed at five different sites in the Valley. When these plants are completed, nuclear power will be the dominant program technology, accounting for 46.4 percent of total generating capacity as compared to 38.1 percent for coal, 10.2 percent for hydroelectric, and 5.3 percent for combustion turbine. The problems that the TVA confronted during the decade are related to three factors: (1) the thermal pollution problem; (2) the coal problem; and (3) a rise in opposition to nuclear power within the Valley.

Thermal Pollution

Opponents of the TVA's nuclear power program have focused primarily on the thermal-pollution problem.[9] When the National Environmental Policy Act (1970) was signed into law, it provided environmentalist and antinuclear forces an important weapon for slowing construction of, and increasing the cost of, nuclear plants.

The TVA's primary opponent in the thermal-pollution controversy was the Environmental Protection Agency (EPA). This controversy is probably best viewed in terms of two federal agencies striving to achieve conflicting goals. Although neither agency opposed the other's goal, implementation of measures to achieve its own goals hindered the goal attainment of the other agency. The EPA was concerned that the thermal pollution from the TVA's nuclear power plants would upset the ecological balance of the bodies of water into which the TVA dumped its heated water discharge. The TVA, on the other hand, perceived the cost of the cooling towers the EPA wanted installed as an unnecessary expense that would add to the rates it would have to charge its power customers.

The TVA capitulated to the EPA's demands only when it became obvious that the goal of providing adequate quantities of electricity was in peril as a result of the EPA's ability, through the National Regulatory Commission (NRC) licensing hearings, to slow the construction and licensing of the TVA's nuclear power plants. The plants, which were already behind their original construction schedules were needed to meet rapidly increasing demands for electricity. The choice, according to TVA officials, was an unnecessary increase in the cost of electricity to TVA customers or power brownouts (*Chattanooga Time*, 1973). They opted for the former.

The Coal Situation

Although the TVA was the focus of much criticism for its role as the nation's largest consumer of strip-mined coal, the principal coal-related problem it experienced in the 1970s concerned air pollution. In mid-1972, the EPA directed the TVA to reduce the level of sulfur dioxide (SO_2) emissions at its eight largest coal-fired steam plants. The date of compliance was set by the EPA as July, 1975, for two of the plants and July, 1977, for the other six. Controversy arose over how the standards would be met. TVA officials wanted to install extremely high smoke stacks that would disperse the pollutants over a large area, stating that at no point on the ground would EPA clean-air standards be violated. The EPA countered with a demand the agency install scrubbers, a technology the TVA considered both unproven and costly. The $1 billion the TVA estimated it would have to expend to install scrubbers was ten times the cost it estimated for tall stacks. When the EPA became adamant in its demand that the TVA install scrubbers, the TVA refused, asserting that the authority to require the use of a specific method in the meeting of clean-air standards was vested in the states. In 1976, the TVA and EPA reached a compromise on some of the TVA's smaller plants, allowing for tall stacks on some units and scrubbers at others. The dispute over the larger plants continued.

A compromise was not worked out until 1978, when the TVA was again confronted with threats of having to cut operations at some of its plants. Alabama and Kentucky state governments, the EPA, and ten citizen groups had filed suit against the TVA in 1977. The compromise that was reached required the TVA to use large quantities of medium- and low-sulphur coal and install a variety of emission-cleaning devices. The TVA estimated the cost of these actions would exceed $400 million a year throughout the 1980s (*Tennessee Valley Authority Annual Report*, 1979).

The Nuclear-Power Controversy

Citizen groups' opposition to the TVA's use of nuclear energy did not become a problem for the agency until 1974 when safety became a rallying point in the TVA service area. This issue, dominant in other areas of the country, had not been a major concern with the Tennessee Valley. TVA officials attribute this to residents of the area "being used to nuclear technology" and willing to "trust in TVA." The Oak Ridge facilities, which produced the first atomic bomb and remain the center of much defense work in the nuclear field, are in the heart of the TVA service area. Thus, residents of the Valley have had over three decades to become acclimated to the presence of nuclear power.

Small but vocal groups formed in all the areas of the TVA's nuclear power plants. Although these citizen groups are small, TVA officials are cognizant of their members' complaints and fears. Several officials mentioned during interviews that these groups were often a focal point of discussion among high-level TVA personnel. Virtually every official who discussed the problem, however, attributed a narrowness of outlook to the members of these groups. In the words of one official, "They aren't the ones responsible when the lights go out; they won't ever have to account for increased unemployment when industry has to shut down because there isn't enough electrical energy."

Unified Resource Development

The goal of the TVA today, as articulated by seventeen high-level officials during interviews in 1977, is "unified resource development." However, there was unanimous agreement that the best way to accomplish this goal was through the provision of "low-cost electrical energy in ample quantity." When, exactly, this interpretation of the agency's goal became accepted, is impossible to say.

Although one cannot generalize from a single case study with any degree of assurance, this analysis of the TVA can be used to suggest propositions about the relationship between organizational goals and the implementation process, which may be tested under a variety of different circumstances. The most obvious proposition concerns the nature of the interrelationship between goals and implementation. Although theories of incrementalism predict such a relationship, they do not accurately depict what has occurred at the TVA. Lindblom (1959; Braybrooke and Lindblom, 1963) describes incremental change as, in part, a process of mutual adaptation where means and ends are repeatedly changed to be brought closer in line with each other. Although the early history of the TVA could be offered as an example of this process, development beyond the first few years defies description from the incremental perspective.

Specifying TVA's goal to be unified resource development through the provision of low-cost electrical energy in ample quantity was, in part, an adaptation to the fact that the means of producing electrical power had become increasingly prominent within the agency. After the early development of the goal, however, the agency continually implemented policies that were meant to accomplish the goal—not adapt it to available means. The TVA's expansion into the areas of coal-fired and nuclear technologies, which holding its goal constant, supports the following proposition:

P1: *The implementation of nonincremental change is facilitated by the establishment of clearly defined organizational goals and the support of organizational leaders for those goals.*

A second proposition, concerning which actors determine the goals of an organization, can be drawn from the first part of the description here of the TVA. Although models of the implementation process assert that the legislative mandate of the organization must distinguish exactly what this goal is, the TVA has demonstrated that bureaucratic organizations can themselves turn nebulous statements of intent into concrete goals. As the TVA forged its goal, the organizational resources necessary to achieve it were diverted to implementation processes that would optimize the possibility of it being achieved. That is, as the goal of providing low-cost electrical energy in ample quantity rose in prominence, so did the power program.

P2: *The possibility of successful implementation, that is, the ability of the organization to achieve its goal, is enhanced by allowing the implementing organization some discretion in choosing its goal.*

An important limiting factor is obviously the discretion TVA had in choosing its own goal. Although much internal conflict occurred before the goal emerged, the agency had an inordinate amount of discretion relative to Congress, the president, and its own history. The TVA was not asked to either carry out the functions or overcome the burdens of an organization that had failed, as was the U.S. Postal Service when it acquired the problems and debts of the U.S. Post Office Department. The TVA's discretion, furthermore, was aided by the era in which it was established. The Great Depression made the country and government willing to experiment and, thus, accept behavior they would not have during more normal times.

P3: *Goals are more likely to be attained if policies are implemented by new organizations rather than established ones.*

P3 is, for political reasons, most appropriate when new problems arise. Old organizations, especially large ones, generally cannot be terminated and replaced by newer ones. Thus, the relevant choice in such situations will be between establishing a new organization or assigning implementation responsibility to an already established organization.

Another factor limiting an agency's success is the amount of discretion it can exercise over the means by which policy will be implemented. In the case of the TVA, discretion has been most obvious in the exclusion of private industry from the service area, and in the expansion into coal-fired and nuclear technologies. Although policy drift in both implementation means and goal is generally viewed in a negative light, it is doubtful the TVA could have success-fully implemented its policies without it. Obviously, if the TVA had been forced to coexist with private industry and had been limited to hydroelectric dams for generating electricity, it could not have sold electricity at low rates or in ample quantity. Therefore, a fourth proposition can be stated:

P4: *Goals are more likely to be attained if organizations are given dis-cretion over the means by which they implement policy.*

The unfortunate dilemma for policymakers, as seen in P3 and P4, is that one may have to be willing to accept either drift in means and goals or implementa-tion failure.

A final proposition concerns a distinct negative aspect of the relationship between organizational goals and the implementation process. When the organ-ization has a clearly defined goal that guides its implementation process, there are potential negative consequences for bureaucratic responsibility. TVA of-ficials, while pursuing the agency's goal, have done so with little deference to forces in the environment. Its establishment of a monopolisitc power program, expansion to include coal-fired steam plants, and rapid development of the nation's largest nuclear-power program, were done in the face of attempts from various outside forces to alter these implementation practices. The fact that opposition has generally met with failure does not mean that the TVA is ir-responsible. Rather, its responsiveness has been to its goal more than to forces in its environment. Indeed, when forces in the environment were capable of inhibiting the TVA's ability to accomplish its goal, implementation practices were altered to appease these same forces. The TVA capitulated on the issue of installing cooling towers and scrubbers when agency officials feared their plants would be limited in operation or even shut down.

P5: *Organizations that have clearly articulated goals to which their leaders subscribe, will respond to external pressures to change their implementation practices only when their goals are threatened.*

The implementation process has been subject of much attention in recent years. A myriad of factors that influence the level of implementation success and failure have been revealed. The intricacies of the relationships between im-plementation and these various influencing factors are just beginning to draw at-tention. It is hoped this chapter has shed some light on one of these relationships.

Notes

1. TVA is deemed successful because of its ability to achieve its goal of providing low-cost electrical energy in ample quantity. See George E. Rawson,

"The Implementation of Public Policy by Third-Sector Organizations" (Prepared for delivery at the 1978 annual meeting of the American Political Science Association, New York, August 31–September 3, 1978).

2. The other principal programs of the TVA concern flood control and agriculture.

3. For a more extensive discussion of the TVA Act from a legal perspective, see Richard Wirtz, "Legal Framework of the Tennessee Valley Authority," *Tennessee Law Review* 43 (Summer, 1976).

4. Harcourt Morgan, the third member of the board, was to oversee the agricultural program.

5. The different views of both men toward the purpose of the TVA and their conflict are discussed in detail in McGraw, *Morgan v. Lilienthal*.

6. The agricultural program was implemented in the opposite fashion of the power program. Morgan chose to enhance the established farming structure rather than supplant it. See Philip Selznick, *TVA and the Grass Roots* (Berkeley: University of California Press, 1949).

7. For a discussion of how the TVA increased the demand for electricity in the Valley, see Victor C. Hobday, *Sparks at the Grassroots* (Knoxville: University of Tennessee Press, 1969).

8. This conflict between the TVA and the private power companies is discussed in detail in Aaron Wildavsky, *Dixon-Yates: A Study in Power Politics* (New Haven: Yale University Press, 1962).

9. Thermal pollution is caused by the rise in water temperature a body of water experiences when hot water is dumped into it. Although fossil-fuel plants create thermal pollution, much of the excess heat from these plants is discharged into the air. At a nuclear-power plant, however, all of the excess heat is discharged into the water.

References

Annual Report of the Tennessee Valley Authority and Appendixes for the Fiscal Year Ended June 30, 1934. Washington, D.C.: United States Government Printing Office, 1935, p. 4.

Braybrooke, David, and Lindblom, Charles E. *A Strategy of Decision.* New York: The Free Press, 1963.

Chattanooga Times. September 18, 1973.

Knoxville News-Sentinel. July 21, 1966.

Lindblom, Charles E. "The Science of Muddling Through." *Public Administration Review* 19 (Spring, 1959): 79–88.

Memphis Commercial Appeal. March 29, 1966.

McGraw, Thomas K. *Morgan v. Lilienthal: The Feud within the TVA*. Chicago: Loyola University Press, 1970, p. 5.

_____. *TVA and the Power Fight, 1933-1939*. Philadelphia: J.B. Lippincott Company, 1971, chap. 1.

National Environmental Policy Act of 1970, Pub. L. No. 91-190, January 1, 1970, 83 Stat. 852, 452 U.S.C. Sections 4321-4347 (1970).

Owen, Marguerite. *The Tennessee Valley Authority*. New York: Praeger Publishers, 1973.

Pritchett, C. Herman. *The Tennessee Valley Authority: A Study in Public Administration*. Chapel Hill: University of North Carolina Press, 1943, p. 73.

Sabatier, Paul, and Mazmanian, Daniel. "The Conditions of Effective Implementation: A Guide to Accomplishing Policy Objectives." *Policy Analysis* 5 (Fall, 1979): 481-504.

Tennessee Electric Power Co. v. T.V.A. 306 U.S. 188, 59 S.C. 366, 83L. ed. 543 (1939).

Tennessee Valley Authority. *Comparison of Coal-fired and Nuclear Power Plants for the TVA System*. Chattanooga, Tenn.: Tennessee Valley Authority, Office of Power, 1966, p. 3.

Tennessee Valley Authority Annual Report, 1978. Knoxville: Tennessee Valley Authority, Vol. 2, 1978, p. 9.

Tennessee Valley Authority Annual Report, 1978. Knoxville: Tennessee Valley Authority, 1979, p. 21.

TVA Act of 1933, sec. 11.

Van Meter, Donald S., and Van Horn, Carl E. "The Policy Implementation Process: A Conceptual Framework." *Administration and Society* 6 (February, 1975): 445-487.

Part II
Implementation Problems

4

Optimizing under CETA: Program Design, Implementation Problems, and Local Agencies

James A. Goodrich

A great deal of effort in public policymaking involves attempts at keeping policies "on course" and in line with legislative intentions. This difficult process is made even harder when federal legislators create programs to be run by local agencies. In such intergovernmental programs, the key seems to be "to design policies and programs that in their basic conception are able to withstand buffeting by a constantly shifting set of political and social pressures during the implementation phase" (Bardach, 1977). When significant gaps emerge between federal policy objectives and actual performance, the legislative strategy often involves strengthening regulations and guidelines and tightening requirements in order to ensure state and local compliance with policy standards. Such efforts frequently accompany reauthorizations in which Congress provides greater specification and clarification of its policy objectives.

The evolution of legislation, amendments, and regulations promulgated for such programs, and the reasons for the changes that have occurred are an important source of information since they reveal problems encountered in the design and implementation of these policies. During the recent reauthorization debates over the Comprehensive Employment and Training Act (CETA), the basic issues were:

1. Which CETA activities have been most effective and how can the good ones be encouraged?
2. How can CETA services be concentrated on people most in need of them (disadvantaged clients, or those with employment difficulties)?
3. How can employment and training funds be targeted on geographic areas with high levels of unemployment?[1]

Reauthorization bill provisions addressed these issues in several ways: by encouraging training activities and employment development programs while putting restrictions on public-service employment (PSE) programs within CETA; by tightening eligibility requirements to target programs on low-income unemployed persons; and by improving allocation formulas through the use of unemployment statistics in order to better identify areas of substantial unemployment.

Such actions reflect the concerns of federal policymakers. Their emphasis has been on better program design and closing loopholes in order to get local job programs to conform to federally stipulated policy objectives. This is typical of legislative debates, as well as more analytical discussions of "optimizing" CETA programs. It would be an exaggeration to claim that these efforts did no good. Certainly they were necessary compromises in order to build political support for the reauthorization effort. But they are likely to be limited in their effects since they do not address any of the real implementation problems that have hampered CETA's effectiveness while making it "the most unpopular program in this country, after welfare."[2]

There is a tendency to define optimality here in terms of designing the best job programs based on our policy goals and our knowledge about what works in achieving them, derived from a model of labor market operations. Yet programs may fail to reach their objectives because of problems of implementation as well as improper design. We may design the perfect program with the clearest goals and strictest regulations, but it still may not work. New targeting restrictions to ensure that only economically disadvantaged participants are enrolled in public-service jobs, for instance, do little good if the PSE buildup is so rapid during a recession that local administrators cannot certify eligibility requirements or find and fill job slots fast enough to meet federal fiscal policy objectives.[3] The implementation problem is compounded, of course, if these local administrators have their own agendas and ideas about how best to use these federal funds.

Experience suggests that major difficulties in getting CETA to work are implementation problems that arise in translating federal goals to locally administered employment and training operations. This chapter concentrates on five problem areas that make such policies far from optimal and result in gaps between federal intentions and local performance. This is not an exhaustive list by any means; the point in looking at such problems is to illustrate that they are not likely to be diminished by current amendments and therefore limit the impact of these improvements in program design.

Multiple, Shifting Objectives

As the name implies, CETA was conceived as a comprehensive act putting together previously disparate manpower programs that had been operating more or less independently. Putting together employment and training programs was intended to ensure better planning and coordination and an improved system for allocating resources. At the same time, program control was shifted to more than 450 state and local units (prime sponsors) in order to decentralize administration and permit flexibility in designing programs to meet different local needs.

The fact that CETA encompasses such a broad range of programs and activities serving different purposes makes it difficult to arrive at any general conclusions about what works best. These programs include on-the-job training, work experience, services for special client groups (such as Indians, migrant workers, youth summer jobs), and public-service employment. As hundreds of prime sponsors put together their own packages of such programs, problems arise in evaluating the combination of activities they choose to pursue, especially since these can be justified in terms of putting together pieces from a variety of programs to deal with local conditions. Federal policymakers have tried to resolve some of this ambiguity by adding new categories of service, specifying different titles to deal with specific problems, and targeting programs more narrowly on particular groups. Such moves toward recategorization have not, however, resolved basic conflicts among multiple program objectives.

As CETA evolved, it continued the structural objectives of earlier programs—emphasizing training aimed at improving the employability of disadvantaged groups—while amendments added emphasized, countercyclical objectives, with PSE jobs created to deal with increasing unemployment. Shifts in emphasis have been extremely rapid. During the last recession, PSE expenditure jumped from 30 percent of total CETA funding during 1975, to approximately 60 percent by 1978. From May 1977 to April 1978, PSE employment grew from 301,000 to 725,000. It is not surprising that in the face of time pressures, both job creation and participant selection were sloppily implemented.[4] A more basic problem was that a single policy was supposed to achieve two different goals: "intended as an economic response to cyclical unemployment, it was, because of social considerations, enlisted to serve structural purposes as well" (Mirengoff and Rindler, 1978, p. 8). Balancing CETA objectives of providing meaningful jobs for hard-core unemployed persons and temporary slots to reduce unemployment implies difficult trade-offs. Local prime sponsors have been given the task of doing both things at once, under conditions of rapid change.

Problems arise in meeting multiple objectives within programs as well. As federal job programs have proliferated in response to the needs of particular groups, CETA targeting efforts have increased. With so many groups being identified for consideration, eligibility requirements have multiplied. This creates practical difficulties for program operators in the selection of participants, since they cannot give equal consideration to all categories at once, and members of one group may not meet other program specifications. As one local administrator put it, "there just aren't that many minority female veterans under 18 around."[5]

Monitoring versus Evaluation

Along with its emphasis on decentralization and local control, CETA legislation assigned the Department of Labor (DOL) a role as overseer. In seeing to it that national objectives were met, the regional offices of the department (RDOL) have been given responsibilities for interpreting national policies, establishing standards for local programs, and assessing prime sponsor performance. As countercyclical objectives were added to CETA, national direction was seen to be even more crucial in order to ensure that state and local governments would be successful agents of federal fiscal policy.

In practice, the major emphasis of the RDOL has been making certain that local program design is in line with federal recommendations and checking compliance of prime sponsors with plans written up to obtain CETA grants. The procedures here revolve around setting up a planned series of target figures under various titles for local programs which are compared to actual performance during program operations. In addition, the RDOL sees to it that hiring procedures for local jobs and other program specifications are consistent with federal requirements.

The thrust of RDOL monitoring efforts are process oriented—that is, they focus on setting up the program, following procedures, maintaining effort, and maintaining percentages of plan achievement. Major concerns in program implementation center on local compliance with minimum federal contract requirements. Quarterly reports are required on cash flows as well as on participant characteristics and performance in achieving planned objectives. Here the major federal role is guarding against financial mismanagement and ensuring that jobs are properly targeted on groups and geographic areas called for by the policy.

The problem with this approach is that the performance indicators do not help in evaluating the merits of various types of programs being funded.[6] This kind of monitoring does very little in estimating the impact of programs being run by prime sponsors for various groups of unemployed and economically disadvantaged clients in their jurisdictions. Overall there is little evidence that the performance measures being used in CETA reports to the RDOL relate to favorable outcomes—placement in good jobs, better earnings, and increased proportion of time in employment. An extensive follow-up study of CETA program participants recently concluded that:

> Most of the present set of [indicators] are poor predictors of program impact . . . Many of the measures presently being used bear little relation to the programs' outcomes. Their continued use will yield allocation decisions that are little (if any) better than decisions made by flipping a coin. (Borus, 1978, p. 13)

If we cannot begin to assess the relative effectiveness of different types of programs or service delivery in order to figure out which ones work better under certain conditions, grave problems in policy implementation arise. Prime sponsors seeking to optimize the use of their resources do not get much guidance in deciding what kinds of programs to support.

Moreover, this kind of monitoring by federal authorities focuses attention on compliance and does very little to help in resolving local management problems and strengthening their operations. For all the efforts to ensure enrollment of the right percentages of disadvantaged participants and adherence to administrative regulations, very little has been done to improve local job-training programs. Yet this is the key to successful implementation of CETA policies. Even if job content, hiring and training procedures, and targeting are consistent with federal regulations, this does not ensure good performance or positive outcomes.

Formulas, Not Incentives

There are few incentives built into this system for prime sponsors to do more than meet minimum federal requirements. The basis for allocating CETA funds between titles and among prime sponsors is a complex formula based on relative state and local shares of total unemployment.[7] This means that the figures used for allocations are beyond the control of the RDOL or the prime sponsors. The amount of funding that is likely to flow to local areas is not really affected by prime-sponsor performance. Once they know that funds are available under the formula, local officials have only to ensure that their applications meet federal specifications to win RDOL approval for federal grants.

Although the RDOL has the power to reject grant applications from prime sponsors with poor performance records, they seldom do so (except in cases of obvious fraud or violation). To do this might limit the extent to which CETA funds get to areas of high unemployment and this is counter to governmental antirecessionary objectives. Also, such actions might mean layoffs of carefully-targeted program participants. So, where high costs or poor placement rates are shown on their quarterly reports, prime sponsors do not suffer funding cutbacks as a result. They are told basically to "try harder."[8]

If the RDOL cannot punish, neither can it reward good performance. The discretionary funds available to the RDOL for allocation on a basis other than unemployment statistics constitute only a small share of total funding. Most of these discretionary funds are used to "hold harmless" prime sponsors (that is, ensure stability in funding arrangements by making sure prime sponsors get at least 90 percent of their previous year's allocation). Such funds are seldom used to reward management improvements or program innovations. Of course, even if they had more discretion over funding, it would be difficult for the RDOL to establish an effective rewards system. "Grading" prime-sponsor performance, even on the basis of limited information generated by quarterly indicators, is difficult since each local unit runs a different combination of programs and there are significant variations in local labor markets and clients being served.[9]

Communication Problems

Increasing the statistical data required in the reporting process to include more relevant performance figures might not improve the situation, given the communications problems between federal and local authorities. Many implementation difficulties have been attributed to the problem of gaining control over a massive flow of information generated by the hundreds of prime sponsors and their estimated 100,000 subcontractors (National Commission, 1978).[10] Local inaccuracies in reporting and the lack of adequate RDOL staff and technical assistance have been noted as major reasons for the lack of accountability and direction in the fragmented and rapidly expanding CETA system (Van Horn, 1978).

Moreover, interpretation of these data on local employment and training operations requires expertise in manpower planning as well as experience in working with local administrators. These qualities are in short supply especially given the complexity of different programs and the high turnover rates among regional office staff and federal representatives assigned to each prime sponsor (Mirengoff and Rindler, 1978). Persistent tensions between prime sponsors and the federal establishment are not likely to be eased by the steady stream of memos, directives, and regulations now flowing from the RDOL demanding more information on the conduct of local programs.

Local Perspective

The major source of federal-local tensions is the legislative ambiguity in CETA related to the limits of local control and federal oversight. Adding to these implementation problems is the divergence between federal and local objectives. Over the years, local administrators have become rather sophisticated "CETA watchers," seeking to gain more control over growing federal job programs while meeting local political demands. The situation is complicated by the fact that prime sponsors (cities, counties, consortia) have become important fixtures within the structure of local governments, and they provide services to client constituencies that have been highly organized since the 1960s. Within CETA's multiple legislative provisions, local administrators have developed their own agendas for putting together local employment and training packages. Generally they have sought to maximize federal grants to their jurisdictions while preserving administrative discretion in using these funds.

From a local perspective, the enactment of CETA Title VI and the subsequent expansion of PSE programs within a short time period brought financial windfalls as the recession deepened and unemployment remained high. Despite the countercyclical goals of these programs, larger and poorer cities became more and more dependent on them.[11] In the face of Proposition 13 and similar revenue-liimitation proposals across the country, many more localities have come to rely on CETA funds for a purpose never intended by the authorizing legislation—fiscal relief. Widespread substitution has occurred as local governments use PSE slots for positions they would have paid for themselves, thus using CETA funds to meet their own payrolls. State and local governments have become major lobbyists for stabilizing PSE funding, making it much harder to "turn off the tap" or cut the flow of antirecessionary assistance as the economy fluctuates. Obviously such substitution is suboptimal in terms of CETA job-creation objectives, though it is hard to measure its extent or its effects.[12]

Limits to Federal Reforms

Efforts of federal policymakers to improve employment and training policies are reflected in the reauthorization amendments to CETA legislation. This approach to better program design—defining limits and objectives more clearly to see to it that funds go to the "best" programs (or limiting expenditures on "bad" ones) and that these funds find their way into the hands of the most needy people in hard-pressed areas—has a long and honorable tradition. With each new round of regulation writing, we see efforts to take account of problems that have emerged, to limit actions by local governments that counter the intent of original legislation, and to design funding arrangements and allocation formulas in a more optimal fashion. Such improvements in program design, however, do not necessarily result in more optimal programs because they do not deal adequately with implementation problems like those just outlined. Indeed it is unlikely that even the best-designed policies will be successfully carried out under these conditions.

Tighter restrictions to reduce the leeway of local prime sponsors in using CETA funds do not help resolve the problem of basically contradictory objectives within CETA. Provisions designed to cut down on local job substitution within PSE programs, such as limiting salaries to near minimum wage, tying jobs to short-term projects, and setting an eighteen-month limit for individual participation, will enhance countercyclical goals. However, these amendments also minimize the opportunities for on-the-job training and preparation for future employment. Tougher eligibility standards to target these temporary jobs for the hard-core unemployed may not help them with the problems. It is difficult to imagine a worse combination than targeting PSE jobs for those with structural difficulties, yet this is an outcome that is predictable given the basic differences between these two objectives and the efforts to design programs to serve both purposes.

Improved allocation formulas may result in more money going to areas of high unemployment. However, this does not necessarily make for improved performance, since prime sponsors have not developed effective systems for transition to unsubsidized employment, and these areas still suffer from lack of jobs (U.S. GAO, 1979). Better targeting may result from new eligibility requirements but this does nothing to improve program management. In other words, we take great pains to ensure that local CETA programs enroll appropriate numbers of poor and disadvantaged participants, but we do very little to make sure these are good programs.[13]

Amendments that increased DOL powers to revoke prime-sponsor funds along with more explicit conditions attached to CETA grants would strengthen the hand of federal representatives in checking that local programs meet legislative standards. But without usable sanctions, RDOL enforcement capacity will remain limited. The emphasis is still on prime-sponsor performance in meeting self-defined program objectives in local plans. Better evaluation systems to grade the effectiveness of different programs require measures of program outcomes and improved management information systems at the local level. With even more complex programs under new regulations, much greater RDOL information-processing capacity and expertise is required than has previously been evident. Discretionary funds are still more limited under new funding formulas and, therefore, less is available to be awarded prime sponsors for good performance. There is a lack of incentives for local managers to experiment, to show how they could do more with the same amount of grant dollars. Federal officials in regional offices have been given more investigative authority but have been left with no carrot and no real stick.

Legislative modifications in CETA policies may serve a useful purpose in clarifying the federal role and specifying goals more clearly. These changes may be necessary especially where program decisions have been left to local authorities who have their own ideas about the "optimal" uses of federal funds for job programs. Where prime sponsors adapting to local pressures deviate from federal policy standards, the original thrust of CETA programs may be lost or watered down in the implementation process. More restrictive legislation, however, is not sufficient to deal with problems encountered in delivering CETA services. In fact, to the extent that these compliance activities add to the responsibilities of already overburdened state and local administrators, they may place additional strains on the CETA system and divert resources away from needed program improvements.

Although CETA reauthorization efforts have sought to restore more control to federal officials, the inescapable fact is that local prime sponsors continue to have significant managerial and operational responsibilities in actually running these programs. In the absence of clear performance measures and enforceable sanctions, local organizations will continue to have discretion in executing CETA policies. The actions of local agencies in dealing directly with program participants basically determine whether employment and training policies succeed or fail. In the future, less emphasis on program designs that ensure tighter control over resources, and more federal support for improving local staff capability may be crucial to better performance. The stimulation of management improvements at the prime-sponsor level should be supplemented by more DOL efforts to encourage innovation by offering incentive funds or underwriting experiments with new approaches to skill training and employability development. More attention to these kinds of implementation issues is the real key to "optimizing" under CETA.

Notes

1. Congressional Budget Office (CBO), *CETA Reauthorizatin Issues* (Washington, D.C. 1978).

2. Congressman David R. Obey, (Democrat, Wisconsin) made this comment in proposing cuts in CETA PSE wages. See *CQ 1978 Almanac* (Washington, D.C.: Congressional Quarterly, Inc., 1978), p. 297.

3. Harry Katz and Michael Wiseman, "An Essay on Subsidized Employment in the Public Sector," in *Job Creation through Public Service Employment* (Washington, D.C.: 1978). National Commission for Manpower Policy.

4. See CBO, *Reauthorization,* p. 3, 19. See also U.S. General Accounting Office (GAO), *Information on the Buildup in Public Service Jobs* (Washington, D.C., 1978).

5. From a personal interview with a staff member of a local prime sponsor. In conducting the research upon which this chapter is based, the author has benefited greatly from interviews with representatives of six California prime sponsors in Region 9.

6. Of course, these figures can be revealing. For instance, reports that suggested widespread "skimming" (choosing those eligibles who are easiest to place in employment and training slots, rather than those most in need of service) occurred during the early years of CETA operations have led to tightening of eligibility requirements. Also these indicators show costs of programs and placements over time and the differences between regions.

7. A major implementation issue here involves problems in getting reliable estimates of unemployment in local areas. According to the U.S. GAO, many problems exist in the estimating process. See U.S. GAO, *Reliable Unemployment Estimates: A Challenge for Federal and State Cooperation* (Washington, D.C., 1979).

8. This not to say that prime sponsors have not had funding cutoffs or been required to return funds in cases of program abuses, but rather, to point out that no prime sponsor has suffered a loss of funding because of low performance ratings.

9. For a good discussion of the problem of comparing performance using these indicators, see U.S. Department of Labor, Employment and Training Administration, *The Implementation of CETA in Eastern Massachusetts and Boston* (Washington, D.C.: R and D monograph no. 57, 1978), pp. 85–87.

10. Of course, an improved management information system for program evaluation could improve this situation somewhat, since much of the burden here is imposed by current requirements that focus more on plans and intentions than on results.

11. According to a recent Treasury Department study, the 48 largest U.S. cities have come to rely heavily on antirecessionary funds, which provide 21 percent of their total federal aid. More than two-thirds of these funds came through CETA PSE and public-service jobs under the Public Works Employment Act. See U.S. Department of Treasury, Office of State and Local Finance, *Report on the Impact of the Economic Stimulus Package on 48 Large Urban Governments* (Washington, D.C., 1978).

12. A good discussion of substitution effects, which includes a review of the results of earlier econometric studies of fiscal substitution, can be found in Michael Borus and Daniel S. Hamermesh, "Study of the Net Employment Effects of Public Service Employment—Econometric Analyses," in *Job Creation through Public Service Employment, vol. 3,* pp. 89-149. Although there is wide variation in estimates of the extent of fiscal substitution, almost all analysts agree it is less likely when wage rates are set low and eligibility criteria are stringent.

13. Of course, the newly created Office of Management Assistance in CETA may help in improving program management; but this still represents only a tiny fraction of total outlays for these employment and training programs.

References

Bardach, Eugene. *The Implementation Game.* Cambridge, Mass.: MIT Press, 1977, p. 5.

Borus, Michael. "Indicators of CETA Performance," *Industrial and Labor Relations Review* (October, 1978): 2, 13.

Mirengoff, William, and Rindler, Lester. *CETA: Manpower Programs under Local Control.* Washington, D.C.: National Academy of Sciences, 1978, pp. 8, 89-90.

National Commission for Manpower Policy. *An Assessment of CETA.* Washington, D.C., 1978, p. 8.

U.S. Government Accounting Office. *Moving Participants from Public Service Employment Programs into Unsubsidized Jobs Needs More Attention.* Washington, D.C., 1979.

Van Horn, Carl. "Implementing CETA: The Federal Role," *Policy Analysis* (Fall, 1978): 177-179.

5 Political Power and Policy Formulation, Implementation, and Evaluation

Beryce W. MacLennan

Public policy affects the allocation of resources and the lives and futures of people with differing cultural values and competing vested interests. Consequently, at every step in the processes of policy formulation, implementation, and evaluation, political forces come into play. This chapter discusses the role of political power in implementing and evaluating.

Political activity is discussed on two levels. One relates to the formal legislative process—attempts to influence policy and programmatic decisions through impacting on the legislature. The second relates to power maneuvers designed to affect the implementation of policies and the distribution of resources necessary for the achievement of program goals.

Public policy is not formulated, legislated, and implemented on the basis of rationality and fact alone, but as a result of the interplay of political power, cultural values, competing priorities, and the known facts about problems and solutions. At each stage of implementation—in the appropriation of funds, establishment of regulations, adoption of standards, and transformation of policy into operating programs in the community—there are continuing battles and shifting coalitions among political, legal, provider, consumer, and community groups with a wide variety of vested interests and values.

Factual and political information is never complete. As policy is implemented, new problems are encountered and adaptations in implementation have to be made. Consequently, evaluations need to be designed dynamically to identify and analyze focal points of conflict and the means of resolving them. Further, it must be recognized that all plans for change have unanticipated consequences, and problems will require redefinition and reanalysis as progress is made.

Although one tends to think of evaluations as impartial and unbiased, they too are affected by the personal values and interests of evaluators and the political power and interests of the sponsor funding evaluation as well as by the constituencies potentially affected by the results (Weiss, 1973). Evaluators will not consider some questions because they are not within the realm of political feasibility.

The opinions in this paper are exclusively those of the author and do not necessarily reflect the views of the U.S. General Accounting Office.

Most descriptions of evaluation technology related to policy development, implementation, and program planning in the mental-health fields address two dimensions—needs assessment and resource availability (Warheit, Bell, and Schwab, n.d.). There is rarely any discussion of the analysis of the dynamic shifts of the identities, roles, functions, power, and financial interests of individuals, groups, and institutions as policy changes are implemented, although some post hoc descriptions have been written. There is usually little analysis of the strategies and tactics required to achieve systems change, or efforts to identify key decision makers supportive or antagonistic toward program goals (Landsberg et al., 1979).

Once a needs and resource assessment has been performed and specific program goals delineated, other steps must be taken in order to address the dynamic forces promoting or constraining policy implementation (Halpert, Horvath, and Young, 1970). It is necessary to make a critical path analysis and to examine the nature of the decisions that must be made in order to achieve each action step. How will the decision be made? Who is likely to be involved in the decision? Who will be affected by the changes? Who will be for the changes and who will be against them? What are the relative power forces and how can the balance of power be changed in a favorable direction? Will it be necessary to develop strategies to try to change opinions and positions of individuals and groups or alter the balance of forces through activating neutral forces?

In implementing a program, we must identify the key decision makers who will influence the development of the program, provide resources, and appropriate funds. Senior executives, legislators, professional elites, and influential citizens must be brought to work in concert to further the program. Sometimes this can be achieved directly; other times coalitions of interest groups may be able to influence governors or legislators. Advisory councils or grass roots advocacy groups may be stimulated to lobby for the program. Negotiations will be necessary to hammer out compromises between differing interest groups. New mechanisms to coordinate or expedite actions will have to be created. A campaign of public education may be necessary to increase public acceptance and reduce opposition to particular plans.

The role of the evaluator is seen as that of companion to manager; to gather data essential for planning, implementing, and monitoring the program; to evaluate the conceptualization of goals and the relevance of strategies and actions; to monitor progress; and to identify when unexpected contingencies are developing and the program is not able to move ahead according to plan.

This chapter describes the care and treatment of handicapped individuals to illustrate the political and power forces that are brought into play as attempts are made to plan for and implement the policy. Strategies, tactics, methods, and techniques necessary to achieve change will be discussed in relation to specific problems.

The phrase *the chronically mentally handicapped* in this chapter refers to individuals who have been deinstitutionalized from a state mental hospital but who are unable to live independently in the community.

Professional and Political Forces That Led to the Adoption of Deinstitutionalization as a Policy

Henry Foley (1975) in his analysis of the events leading to the Community Mental-Health Center (CMHC) Act of 1963, demonstrates clearly the strategies adopted by a small group of men and women to realize a policy of moving patients out of institutional care into care and treatment in the community. They capitalized on advances in medical treatment, particularly psychopharmacology, and on the need for improved psychiatric treatment. They formed a coalition of medical scientists, key congressional politicians, and philanthropists. Through funding of mental-health grants for research and demonstration, they were able to create constituencies in major universities and to increase the number of mental-health professionals working in communities. Support was also obtained through the creation of the National Advisory Council of the National Institute of Mental Health (NIMH), composed of eminent professionals, scientists, citizens, and ex officio representatives of professional organizations.

The philanthropists in the group supported hiring a lobbyist and promoted public education to reduce the stigma of mental illness through their actions. Public opinion gradually became more tolerant of the treatment of the mentally handicapped in the community and more outraged at the conditions in mental institutions.

The Joint Commission on Mental Illness and Health, whose membership overlapped with that of the National Advisory Council, was also created. This commission included membership from all major constituencies concerned with mental health. Its final report, "Action for Mental Health," was published by the American Legion in 1960 in order to reduce opposition from the right. This report, among other things, recommended that mental hospitals be reestablished as mental-health centers providing integrated community services, including inpatient, outpatient, and aftercare services. It also recommended that federal, state, and local governments should share in the cost of services to the mentally ill.

But compromises had to be made. According to Foley (1975), for sufficient support of the centers to become a reality, it was necessary to provide mental-retardation programs with separate administration and their own funding. The staffing of community mental-health centers was delayed until the fears of the American Medical Association and the American Psychiatric Association that psychiatrists would be prevented from private practice were allayed. This was achieved when federal third-party, fee-for-service reimbursement was assured through titles 18 and 19 of the Social Security Act.

Prior to the adoption of the policy of deinstitutionalization, most chronically mentally handicapped individuals were maintained under custodial care in isolated institutions far from their native communities and families. They were able to maintain few if any connections with their previous lives. Most funds for the mentally handicapped were supplied by state governments and went to support these institutions. These funds not only provided for all the care and treatment necessary to maintain the institutionalized patients but also served to employ large numbers of maintenance, custodial, and direct-care workers. These institutions for the mentally handicapped provided economic support for local communities in which the staffs lived. Even when inmates were released from the institutions the hospital staff continued to follow and care for them in the community. This mutually supportive system was threatened when moves were made in earnest to treat patients in the community and to shift staff, money, and other resources to meet their needs there.

Initially, there was a lack of recognition that as one moved these patients out of "total" institutions into the community, all their needs had to be provided for. It also was barely recognized that the influx of a new population into a town or city affects the environment, makes new demands on the community, and that, consequently, local government must become involved.

If a complete analysis of the steps and changes necessary to achieve large-scale deinstitutionalization had been made, the involvement of state and local government officials would probably have been predictable. As patients move out into the community the same number of workers are no longer needed in the institutions and they must follow the patients, retire, or move elsewhere. Inevitably there was a move by state employees to organize. In some states the unions played a major role in protecting the interests of their membership.

State legislators have to consider that positions and budgets must be moved to the community or funds freed to be used elsewhere, and land and facilities owned by the state must be turned to other purposes or sold off. State legislators must also be concerned about the citizens in the communities that receive the patients.

In Massachusetts, an association of ex-mental patients became a vocal force in lobbying for community resources to aid in deinstitutionalization. In 1978, the NIMH published a pamphlet on the values and activities of self-help groups and at the 1980 National Council of Community Mental Health Center's annual conference, almost twenty sessions were devoted to working with boards and advocacy groups and involving citizens in program evaluation.

As the failure to provide for patient needs in the community became more apparent, the force of the law and the criminal justice system came into play in two ways. First, lawyers and professionals, on behalf of handicapped and institutionalized individuals, began to seek treatment and freedom for patients through the courts. Judges began to mandate conditions of treatment in the institutions and to state that patients could not be held in state institutions unless treatment was provided. Second, some patients, insufficiently supported in the community, were considered public nuisances, charged with disorderly conduct or other misdemeanors and they began to be channeled into the criminal justice system. This aroused the concerns of citizens and overtaxed the correctional systems.

The move to deinstitutionalize the handicapped requires not only the transfer of existing resources, but also the creation of new administrative structures at the state level. In Massachusetts, for example, it was necessary to persuade the legislators who controlled the financing of staff positions to agree to line-item changes. The state personnel system was old-fashioned and not equipped to accommodate new types of workers. Any changes had to be worked out with the personnel administrator and the legislative ways and means committees. An adequate data collection system had to be developed. A sufficient coalition of allies within the legislature had to be created to effect these changes, and to obtain this coalition, broad-based citizen support had to be obtained. Citizen support was enlisted through the creation of state advisory boards as well as through the traditional mental-health associations and through a state commission established as a planning task force.

Residential Change

When deinstitutionalization occurs, new facilities and semiprotected housing for the handicapped have to be developed in the community. If this is not achieved, transfer often cannot be made and individuals remain in the institution or are placed in unsuitable lodgings such as flophouses in commercial areas.

One task is to find start-up money for residences, group homes, or cooperative apartment arrangements. A second is to decide where the handicapped will be located. Local residents become concerned about whether neighborhoods will be affected positively or negatively.

In the efforts to obtain funding for housing for the chronically handicapped mental patients, federal legislators broadened the scope of "handicapped" from "physically handicapped" to "handicapped." However, active lobbying by certain handicapped groups and the failure to lobby by the mental-health constituencies (who had not been used to giving consideration to housing in the community) led to the initial exclusion by regulation of the chronically mentally ill from participation in funding, even though others, such as the developmentally retarded, who had lobbied, were included. This illustrates well that the controlling factors in health planning are political, not technical. However, once the problem was recognized, representatives from the National Mental Health Association and state mental-health administrators brought the issue to the attention of the relevant House and Senate committees. In conference, committee members reaffirmed that there was no intent to exclude the mentally handicapped from benefiting from the program to fund housing for the elderly and handicapped. The mental-health constituencies then worked with the Department of Housing and Urban Development and the NIMH to provide demonstration projects for housing for the chronically mentally handicapped in the community and to establish appropriate standards.

At the community level, the struggle not only concerns fiscal matters between competing constituencies for community development and social service money, but also centers on zoning. Citizens may be anxious to preserve the integrity of their neighborhoods, to protect themselves against any reduction in property values, or to protect their children against possible dangers. If so, they may lobby to prevent the establishment of group homes and residences and treatment centers in their neighborhoods. In planning to establish community residences and in selecting neighborhoods, planners must carefully assess the climate of the neighborhood, and develop a strategy for neighborhood acceptance. A recent study shows that some neighborhoods appear to be predictably more receptive than others (Segal, 1980). However, it is still debatable whether it is better to move in fast or to try first to create a friendly group of neighbors who will support the establishment of the facility.

Each type of housing for the handicapped has its own range of funding. For instance, nursing-home beds may be acquired by mental-health constituency efforts only to be filled by the physically handicapped who have been waiting in general hospitals for less costly beds. Bureaucratic coalitions must be developed among health, mental-health, and welfare staffs to work out a reasonable distribution of scarce resources as well as to create procedures for processing applications in a timely fashion (MacLennan, 1976).

Availability of funding may determine placement choices. Whether group residences are developed will depend on the availability of start-up grants or mortgage money. The use of group foster homes depends on working out initial supplemental security income or emergency welfare payments and the stringency of life-safety regulations. Sometimes veterans and civilian handicapped clients compete for the same foster homes.

In Massachusetts, obtaining consent to rent or build mental-health facilities in the community required numerous agreements. Agreement had to be reached not only among the legislature, the local citizenry, and the mental-health professionals and administrators, but also among the state general-service and facility-planning administrators, and in some cases, the health planning agency. Any changes in plan or design usually had to wend their way back and forth through all these groups before final consent could be achieved. This sometimes took years.

In Alabama, Federal District Judge Johnson required the creation of a mental-health authority that had the right to sell state hospital land and buildings and use the money for the development of new mental-health facilities and services. In most states, however, the legislature is unwilling to give up any state land, and even if land is sold, the money is likely to go back into the general fund.

Manpower

When patients move out of the institution, new staff roles and functions are required for crisis teams and emergency management, case management, day-treatment and medication clinics, foster home and group-home management, sheltered workshops, alcoholism programs, nursing-home consultation, re-socialization programs, and the organization of community support groups. Some staff must move from the hospital to be retrained for these jobs, and new staff will be needed.

Staff salaries in state budgets customarily have been funded through annual appropriations. Can the legislature be persuaded to transfer these positions to community budgets? Who will run the community programs? Will the state still provide staff, positions, and salary, or will there be a move to contract out to private groups or even to move to a total third-party reimbursement system? Will the union, if the hospital is organized, be supportive? How will seniority affect the possibility of selecting the most suitable staff for different jobs?

In many states, line-item budgets are the rule so that no positions can be changed without the consent of the legislature. This can involve much backstage politicking by incumbents of positions and by those who have held the right to the disposition of the position. If vacant positions are held open, while consent is sought for their transfer to community budgets from the legislature, the latter may abolish them entirely on the grounds that if not used they are not needed; or vacancies may be frozen so that positions in competing fields, such as fire and safety, may be filled.

If positions are abolished and new positions created, there may be many difficulties with antiquated civil-service selection procedures or with unions. Individuals may qualify for jobs who are unable to carry out the new functions. Union regulations may place restrictions on the distance an individual may be required to move to a new job or on the length of shift he may work. All this can seriously hamper change. If compromises are to be made, key individuals must be involved in planning from the start. However, some individuals will never support the change, and ways must be found to move the individual by promotion, transfer, retirement, or job abolition. Such actions obviously mobilize countereffords and may create fierce power battles.

Summary

It is clear that our ability to predict and control the future is limited. Consequently, planning and evaluation must be a dynamic process. As changes occur, new and unexpected conditions and problems occur; these must be assessed and actions must be adjusted to meet the changes. Deinstitutionalization, where it has been successfully accomplished, has led to the creation of a new order of problems. The resources available to meet the needs of individuals once served in one place by one system now come in fragmented fashion from many different sources. A new system must be developed and, in the process, vested interests will be disturbed and power battles will ensue.

Many ex-patients manage to move ahead and to be more self-reliant, and they regain a level of functioning that would never have been possible in the institution. Others flounder and may end up in a worse state. Concerned individuals—whether citizens, consumers, professionals, bureaucrats, or legislators—must regroup to reassess the existing situation, redefine the problems, and move ahead to the next level of strategy, action, and conflict.

In this analysis, a number of political actions have been identified as critical in the implementation of policy. A power base must be established from which to operate. Key influential figures who can form coalitions to support the provision of resources must be identified and brought together. Coalitions must be formed to speed changes and compromises negotiated between interested parties. In order for a program to succeed, a plan of action should be developed that clearly identifies each point of conflict and designs a strategy to change the balance of power in favor of the plan.

References

Altman, Drew. "The Politics of Health Care Regulation." *Journal of Health Policy and Law* 2, no. 4(1978):560–580.

Attkisson, C. Clifford et al. *Evaluation of Human Services.* New York: Academic Press, 1978.

Bardach, Eugene. *The Implementation Game.* Boston, Mass.: MIT Press, 1977.

Benjamin, A.J., and Levi, A.M. "Process Minefields in Intergroup Conflict Resolution." *Journal of Applied Behavioral Science* 15, no. 4(1979):507–519.

Brown, Bertram; Stockdill, James W.; and Serovotka, Paul J. *The Politics of Mental Health—Update for the 1970s.* Rockville, Maryland, July 1978.

Community Mental-Health Centers Act, PL 88-164, 1963.

Connery, Robert H. et al. *The Politics of Mental Health.* New York: Columbia University Press, 1968.

Foley, Henry A. *Community Mental Health Legislation,* Lexington, Mass.: Lexington Books, D.C. Heath and Company, 1975.

Fry, Brian R., and Thompkins, Mark E. "Some Notes on the Domain of Public Policy Studies." *WHAT*, 1977.

Goldman, William. "Change in a State Department of Mental Health: A View from Within." *Administration in Mental Health* (Fall 1976): 2-9.

Halpert, H.; Horvath, William J.; and Young, John P. *The Application of Operations Research to the Administration of Mental Health Systems.* Washington, D.C.: National Clearinghouse for Mental Health Information, NIMH, 1970.

Heller, Kenneth, and Monahan, John. *Psychology and Community Change.* Dorsey, 1977.

Hirschowitz, Ralph G. "Two Psychiatric Hospitals in Transition." *Hospital and Community Psychiatry* 25, no. 2(1974):730-733.

Housing and the Elderly and Handicapped. PL 93-383, title 20 and section 8, 1978.

Joint Commission of Mental Illness and Health, Action for Mental Health, New York: Basic Books, 1961.

Kilmann, Ralph H. *Social Systems Design.* New York: North-Hollent, 1977.

Landsberg, Gerald et al. *Evaluation in Practice.* Washington, D.C.: Department of Health, Education, and Welfare (ADM), 1979, pp. 78-763.

MacLennan, Beryce W. *Recycling Mental Health Resources.* Rockville, Maryland, 1976.

National Council of Community Mental Health Centers Annual Conference. San Francisco, 1980.

O'Connor v. *Donaldson,* 422 U.S. 563, Slip op. at.

Pressman, Jeffrey, L., and Wildavsky, Aaron. *Implementation.* Berkeley: University of California Press, 1973.

Segal, Stephen. *Community Reactions to the Mentally Ill.* San Francisco: National Council of Mental Health Education, 1980.

Silverman, Phyllis R. *Mutual Help Groups.* Washington, D.C.: DHEM (ADM), 1978, pp. 78-646.

Social Security Act. titles 18 and 19, PL 89-97, July 30, 1965.

Suchman, E.A. *Evaluation Research Principles and Practice in Public Service and Social Action Programs.* New York: Russell Sage, 1967.

Thompson, Frank J. *Personnel Policy in the City: The Politics of Jobs in Oakland.* Berkeley: University of California Press, 1975.

Warheit, George J.; Bell, Robert A.; and Schwab, John J. *Planning for Change: Needs Assessment Approaches.* NIMH Contract NIH-MH-15900-05S1, n.d.

Weiss, Carol. "Where Politics and Evaluation Research Meet." *Evaluation* 1, no. 3(1973):37-45.

6

Conflict over Water-Quality Standards: The Case of Kansas

Marvin A. Harder

Kansas was one of the last states to have its water-quality standards approved by the federal government. Approval came in a letter from William D. Ruckelshaus, administrator, Environmental Protection Agency (EPA), to Governor Robert Docking on 5 May 1971, five years and five months after the enactment by Congress of the Water-Quality Act of 1965. The delay was a result of a conflict between the Missouri Basin office of the federal Water-Pollution-Control Administration (FWPCA) (which in 1970 became a regional office of the EPA) and the Kansas State Board of Health. The principal issue was the federal government's insistence on a 1975 deadline for the construction of secondary waste-treatment facilities for all municipalities discharging effluent into tributaries of the Missouri River. The Kansas State Board of Health finally capitulated when on 8 January 1971, the board adopted, under protest, a new set of regulations to implement the standards and criteria specified by the EPA.

The case is instructive about the conditions that can contribute to delay and controversy in the intergovernmental implementation of a federal policy or program. The case is also instructive in the sense that it suggests a question that is relatively unaddressed in the current literature of policy implementation: When is delay arising from conflict dysfunctional?

The facts presented in this chapter have been selected parsimoniously on the premise that readers will be more interested in the analysis than in the scenario. But they are entitled to know that the first step in this scholarly endeavor was a compiling of more than seventy documents—minutes, letters, memoranda, reports, and newspaper stories and editorials—that reveal the many dimensions of a protracted conflict over water-quality standards in Kansas.[1] This story begins with the adoption by Congress of the Water-Quality Act of 1965. A summary of that decision follows:

The Water-Quality Act

The Water-Quality Act of 1965 amended the federal Water-Pollution-Control Act in several ways:

1. It included in its statement of purpose its intention "to enhance the quality

and value of our water resources and to establish a national policy for the
prevention, control, and abatement of water pollution."

2. It created within the Department of Health, Education, and Welfare a
   federal Water-Pollution-Control Administration.

3. It authorized the secretary to make grants to any state, municipality, or
   intermunicipal or interstate agency for research and development of improved methods of controlling the discharge of sewage into any waters.

4. It increased the authorization of funds to assist in the construction of
   sewage treatment works.

5. It provided a procedure for the establishment of water-quality standards and
   criteria, stipulating that "in establishing such standards the Secretary,
   Hearing Board, or the appropriate State authority shall take into consideration their use and value for public water supplies, propagation of fish and
   wildlife, recreational purposes, and agricultural, industrial and other legitimate uses."

6. It authorized the secretary "after reasonable notice" and a conference of
   appropriate federal, state, and local authorities "to prepare regulations
   setting forth standards of water quality to be applicable to interstate waters
   or portions thereof."

7. It provided for a hearing board and appeal procedure.

In the section relating to the setting of water-quality standards, the act encouraged the governors and state water-pollution-control agencies to take the
initiative by adopting water-quality criteria to be applicable to interstate waters
and by developing a plan for the implementation and enforcement of the water-
quality criteria adopted. These actions are to be reviewed by the secretary, who,
if he finds the state's criteria and plan in accordance with the goals of the act
(protective of the public health and welfare and designed to enhance the quality
of water), shall promulgate such standards.

In contrast to other parts of the act, the section containing guidelines for
approving standards and criteria are quite general and somewhat ambiguous.
The secretary is obligated to consider the "use and value for public water supplies, propagation of fish and wildlife, recreational purposes, and agricultural,
industrial, and other legitimate uses."

Actions and Reactions

Chronologically ordered, the following events occurred.

1. The United States Department of Interior specified the standards it
would seek to enforce in the implementation of the act. The standards included
maximum allowable coliform counts in water supplies and in waters used for
recreational purposes, a maximum allowable dissolved oxygen measure, and a

maximum allowable temperature caused by waste discharges. In addition, all communities on defined waterways would be required to construct secondary waste-treatment plants by 1975 (in Kansas, thirty-two municipalities would be affected by this rule) under penalty of losing federal assistance money if a state failed to comply (at the time, Kansas would have lost $3 million).

2. The Kansas State Board of Health quickly protested the standards on the grounds (1) that they represented federal overriding of a successful state program, (2) that because of the topographical and agricultural nature of the state, they were useless and impossible to attain, (3) that the 1975 deadline for construction of secondary waste-treatment facilities was arbitrary, and (4) that implementation of the standards would impose a costly burden on Kansas citizens. The Board of Health protested directly to the regional director of the federal Water-Pollution-Control Administration and by means of a letter to Secretary Udall signed by the governor of Kansas, Robert Docking.

3. On 16 January 1969, Governor Docking forwarded to Secretary Udall the state's implementation plan and an offer to agree to 1985 as the date for construction of secondary waste-treatment plants.

4. On 18 January 1969, the new Secretary of Interior, Walter Hickel, refused to accept the 1985 date, and 1975 was suggested again.

5. On 9 May 1969, the Kansas State Board of Health decided to stand by the Kansas standards.

6. The following month, the director of Environmental Health Services in Kansas asked the State Board of Health to approve a statement he was planning to present at the Missouri Water-Pollution-Control hearing scheduled for 13 June 1969. He proposed to argue that requirements for waste treatment should be decided on an individual basis as opposed to requiring arbitrary reductions of waste parameters.

7. On 20 June 1969, the president of the State Board of Health, Dr. Kenneth Graham, wrote to Senator James Pearson explaining the board's position and voicing the board's complaints against the federal Water-Pollution-Control Administration.

8. On 27 June 1969, Senator Pearson sent a copy of Dr. Graham's letter to David Dominick, commissioner of the FWPCA, and requested "a detailed response at the earliest possible date."

9. Commissioner Dominick responded with a five-page, single-spaced letter. He began by acknowledging that the mandate of Congress on the federal Water-Pollution-Control Act as amended gives the primary responsibility for preventing and controlling water pollution to the states. "At the same time, he wrote, "the Act does designate certain responsibilities to the Secretary of the Interior and in turn to this agency." Specifically, "the directive to the FWPCA is to assume that water quality will be enhanced and accordingly the policy on treatment requirements was established. . . . We believe the Congressional directive to the FWPCA required us to set a National policy within which

the policies of the individual States would take effect." With respect to the dollar burden of constructing secondary treatment facilities, Commissioner Dominick wrote, "the establishment of positive goals is indeed the prelude to securing public funds for carrying out projects, not the result of availability of funds. We share the concern of State and local authorities about the current stringency of funds for waste treatment works construction. However, today's fiscal situation should not govern planning for the next decade; present fiscal constraints should not limit the establishment of future priorities." Finally, in the matter of duplicating monitoring states, the commissioner justified the new stations as a decision resulting from the need for additional water-quality data.

10. On 12 December 1969, John Rademacher, regional director of the FWPCA, appeared before the State Board of Health to explain his agency's position.

11. At the January 1970 meeting of the State Board of Health, the members heard a report of a study of water quality in the Soldier Creek Basin (an area of about three hundred square miles) in which there are no industries or waste or sewage disposal systems. The study concluded that the pollution levels resulting from runoff of Kansas farmland were above those which federal water-quality standards would permit. This study was subsequently cited by the Environmental Health Division of the State Department of Health as justification of its contention that the construction of secondary facilities on certain streams would not significantly improve water quality.

12. On 30 January 1970, the executive secretary of the State Board of Health, Dr. E.D. Lyman, wrote John Rademacher advising that "the Board wished to delay action on establishing a deadline until thorough legal study can determine the authority of the Board to do so."

13. On 10 February 1970, President Nixon sent Congress a special message that by implication supported the positions of the FWPCA.

14. On 11 February 1970, water-pollution-control officials of the states of Missouri, Iowa, Nebraska, South Dakota, and Kansas met in Omaha to discuss their common problems. Melville Gray reported to the Kansas State Board of Health the consensus that there were many inconsistencies in the federal position and that "future negotiations on water quality control standards should be carried out with the states en masse rather than with individual states."

15. On 31 March 1970, the Missouri Water-Pollution-Control Board reversed its position and advanced the date from 1982 to 1975 for completion of secondary treatment facilities for all municipalities and industries on the Missouri and Mississippi Rivers.

16. Following an appearance before the State Board of Health, Dr. Marvin Harder, special assistant to the governor, sent a memorandum to the governor reporting the substance of his statement to the board. He informed the board that although the governor understood the position taken by Mr. Gray and the board and found merit in their stand, it was the governor's belief that the issue

should be resolved in favor of the federal government's position. It is the federal government that must make the general policies with respect to the protection of our land, water, and air resources. If each state is permitted to go its own way, the result will be that all of us will be victimized by what other states do and do not do. Therefore, unless there were compelling reasons to the contrary, Kansas ought to comply with the federal position.

17. On 20 April 1970, John Rademacher sent a telegram to Dr. Harder. The message read: "The treatment construction schedule called for in the Kansas water quality standards was due December 31, 1969. The Department of the Interior has been faced with a series of delays on the part of the Kansas Board of Health in complying with this condition and the specific exceptions. . . . In the absence of any positive action by the State of Kansas, this office has no alternative but to recommend institution of direct Federal action provided for under Section 10 of the Federal Water Pollution Control Act, as amended."

18. On 4 May 1970, the largest circulation newspaper in the state, *The Wichita Eagle,* editorialized in opposition to what was called a squeeze play. Because the Board of Health was being coerced into acceptance of the federal position by pressure on the one side from the governor's office and on the other from the federal government, it would be the municipalities that in the end would pay. They would be the victims. Secondary sewage treatment plants were not what was needed for cleaner water in Kansas, the paper continued, because most of the state's water pollution comes from land runoff, not from cities. "What Washington doesn't seem to realize is that cities, which are a big factor in water pollution in heavily populated and industrialized regions like the East Coast, are a minor factor here."

19. In June 1970 the State Board of Health was informed that federal construction grants in the sum of $10 million for Kansas were being held up by the secretary of Interior until such time as the water-quality standards are approved.

20. On 9 June 1970, *The Wichita Eagle* followed an earlier editorial by urging the cities of Kansas to protest the fact that the State Board of Health at the request of Governor Docking had "sold the cities down the river." The editorial estimated that federal requirements would cost the cities $10 to $15 million per year. And the article predicted that the State of Kansas would fail to provide the matching funds that would insure that the federal share would equal 55 percent of costs.

21. On 20 June 1970, the *Eagle* published two letters written by Dr. Harder and Mr. Rademacher in response to the June 9 editorial. Dr. Harder defended Governor Docking's decision, contending that "the fact that runoff from fields also pollutes our waterways does not relieve municipalities from their responsibility for contributing to the pollution of streams." Mr. Rademacher charged the editorial writer with advocating "dilution as the solution for pollution."

22. In a memorandum to Governor Docking, dated 17 July 1970, Melville Gray estimated that "the requirements for municipal waste treatment facilities over the next five years indicate 107 cities will be required to expand plants at an estimated cost of approximately $44 million."

23. In a memorandum to officials of certain Kansas cities, E.A. Mosher, executive director of the League of Kansas Municipalities, gave notice of hearings on water-quality standards scheduled for 1 September 1970. He summarized the effects of the proposed regulations as requiring (1) universal secondary treatment facilities, (2) chlorination of effluents, and (3) temperature controls for effluents. He then designated the municipalities that would be affected by each requirement, and estimated the total cost by 1976 to be $43.6 million for secondary facilities, $4 to $5 million for chlorination equipment, $8 million for cooling, plus $3 to $4 million in annual operating costs.

24. On 31 August 1970, in a letter to Dr. Lyman, Governor Docking recommended postponement of the hearings until disagreements or misunderstandings between federal and state officials could be resolved. The hearing was not postponed.

25. At its November meeting, the State Board of Health defeated a motion to retain its existing standards and take whatever action was appropriate after the federal Water-Quality Administration (FWQA) rejected the standards. The board then voted to adopt the standards that had been agreed on by arbitration in a meeting held on 30 September 1970.

26. On 8 January 1971, the State Board of Health voted, under protest, to adopt the regulations on water-quality criteria that conform to U.S. requirements. The board also voted to use the standards developed by the Water-Quality-Control Advisory Council as "implementing guidelines" insofar as possible.

27. On 5 March 1971, in a letter to Governor Docking, William Ruckelshaus approved in their entirety the revised water-quality standards of Kansas.

28. On 8 August 1971, *The St. Louis Post-Dispatch* reported that Jerome H. Svore had replaced John Rademacher as regional administrator, that Rademacher had been replaced at the request of the chairman of the Republican National Committee, Senator Robert Dole, and that "the lesson that there is politics in pollution" is evident. The article further reported that complaints about Rademacher's "insensitivity" and "heavy handedness" were received in Washington from certain industries and from Melville Gray.

29. On 6 January 1972, the U.S. General Accounting Office published its report concluding that the secondary treatment requirement "would result in significant expenditures of public funds which otherwise might be used to meet more pressing water pollution needs." The report noted that "the immediate cause of the decline in dissolved oxygen following periods of heavy rain is that untreated sewage reaches the river because the increased flow through sewer systems exceeds the treatment plant capacities so that the excess flows directly

into the river in an untreated state. Furthermore, the rain results in considerable runoff from the land, carrying pollution from agricultural and construction activities and organic wastes from feedlots into the river." The report ends with the recommendation that the administrator of the EPA "reconsider the timing of the requirement for secondary treatment of municipal wastes along the Missouri River."

Implementation of an Intergovernmental Program

The propositions suggested by this case, along with brief explanatory statements, follow:

P1: *When a federal program preempts an established state program, and contravenes the standard operating procedure of the state agency that administers the program, resistance and delay in implementation are inevitable.*

Two directors of the Environmental Health Services of the Kansas State Board of Health were unwilling to yield the discretionary power they had exercised in the enforcement of state antipollution laws. Federal officials interpreted the Water-Quality Act in a manner that would have required a uniformity in the application of water-quality standards and thereby denied state officials their power to *selectively* mandate antipollution measures. Discretion in administration is the essence of administrative power and is not quickly or easily relinquished.

P2: *The intergovernmental structure through which most federal programs are administered provides political means by which state bureaucrats can resist implementation standards and procedures they do not like.*

The efforts of the chief engineer and director, Melville Gray, to rally his counterparts in the states of the Missouri River Valley, the efforts of the Kansas Board of Health to persuade the United States senators from Kansas to intervene, and the eventual replacement of John Rademacher as the regional administrator of the federal act all demonstrate the significance of federalism as an intervening variable in the implementation of certain federal programs. They also attest to the cogency of Samuel Beer's description of the federal system as a *representative* system.

P3: *A state governor, who exercises appointive and budgetary powers, can terminate delays on the state level in the implementation of federal programs if he chooses to do so, but his decision to intervene in this way will occur only if political considerations make that option more attractive than supporting state-agency resistance.*

Any governor is likely to be predisposed to support a state agency under his authority in its confrontation with a federal agency. Initially, Governor Robert Docking sent federal officials the letters the Board of Health drafted and requested him to sign and send. But in time, other considerations cooled his support of the Board of Health. The chief engineer's statements to the press at times were directly or indirectly critical of the governor and his staff. The Board of Health came to be viewed as unresponsive to the governor's fiscal and other policies; specifically, his view that Kansas officials could not legitimately assert their autonomy in a policy matter that affected the interest of non-Kansans as well as Kansans. The Board of Health's eventual acceptance of federal water-quality standards was a response to the governor's wish that it do so.

P4: *Technical objections to a federal implementation plan, particularly when the technicians at the state level are the implementors, tend to encourage resistance.*

The state engineers' belief, that under conditions devoid of industrial or municipal pollution, natural runoff from fields and pastures could produce coliform counts higher than what federal standards would allow, rationalized their opposition to the proposed federal standards. Technicians tend to be less sensitive or tolerant of political influences in the processes of program implementation than generalists who are accustomed to acting in a political environment.

P5: *Hearings on an implementation plan (often mandated by federal law) provide state bureaucrats an opportunity to mobilize interest-group opposition to specifics of a federal implementation plan and thereby invite delay.*

Feedlot operators, as well as utility executives, manufacturers, and the spokesmen for municipal governments, all had reasons for opposing one or more of the water-quality standards that the federal agencies sought to impose. They became allies of the State Board of Health and buttressed the latter's inclination to resist the federal implementation plan.

In the absence of more case studies focusing specifically on the problems that arise at the state level in the implementation of federal programs, it will be difficult to know whether the propositions presented here are idiosyncratic, that is, unique to the setting of water-quality standards in Kansas.

When Are Implementation Delays Dysfunctional?

If it is difficult to know whether any given program is a failure, it is also diffi-ult to determine when implementation delay is dysfunctional. Although five years of conflict and delay in the implementation in Kansas of the Water-Quality Act of 1965 seems to have been an unacceptable period of time for issues resolu-tion, one might argue that the case simply illustrates the time it may take to formulate policies; that the case is less a study of implementation failure than it is of policy development. Moreover, it could be argued that the resistance to federal water-quality standards was functional if one accepts the State Board of Health's position that technological aspects flawed the federal implementa-tion plan.

If it is assumed that successful implementation means *expeditious* imple-mentation, then policies or programs that are administered intergovernmentally are likely candidates for any list of implementation failures. But if we accept the idea of *reinvention,* that is, changing a program so that it is adaptable to a local setting,[2] and if we recognize that reinvention takes time, then delay may be perceived as the time it takes to negotiate the acceptance of a reinvented implementation plan. From this perspective, delay and the controversies that may attend it make the label of implementation failure inappropriate in certain cases. A delay that is once perceived as dysfunctional may now be perceived as a characteristic of the process of reinvention or, in other words, the process of policy or program formulation.

Notes

1. Marvin Harder, *Selected Papers on the Conflict over Water Quality Standards in Kansas* (unpublished manuscript), May, 1972.

2. Ronald E. Rice, and Everett M. Rogers, "Reinvention in the Innova-tion Process," *Knowledge* 1, no. 4 (Sage Publications, 1980), pp. 500–501.

**Part III
The Implementation-Evaluation
Connection**

7

On the Hazards of Selecting Intervention Points: Time-Series Analysis of Mandated Policies

Michael C. Musheno

Over the last decade, applied researchers have increasingly turned to the interrupted time-series, quasi-experiment to assess the impact of mandated policies and programs. A number of reasons explain applied researchers' growing attachment to this design and its accompanying analytic techniques.

Owing to a host of political constraints, most attempts to evaluate social programs or technologies[1] mandated by law must be post-hoc or unplanned undertakings (Campbell, 1969; Levine, Musheno, and Palumbo, 1980). The time-series design allows scientists to use relevant archival data to study social reforms as near experiments rather than forcing them to await the emergence of an experimenting society willing to choose policies and programs based on scientific research rather than politics. Thus, without delay, contemporary public programs and policies can be translated into field-setting, quasi-experiments through the use of time-series designs.

Also, since applied researchers are most interested in whether a particular public problem (for example, the rate of armed robberies) is ameliorated by a social technology or program (such as gun-control legislation), they are especially attracted to research designs that assure "high internal validity of findings" (Cook and Campbell, 1979, p. 83). They want the greatest assurance possible that the observed effect is indeed attributable to the social program or policy under investigation rather than to an alternative explanation. Since the initial work of Campbell and Stanley in 1963, a number of individuals have developed a checklist of threats to internal validity in field settings (Campbell and Stanley, 1963), Lempert, 1966, pp. 130–132; Glass, Willson, and Gottman, 1975, pp. 53–70; Cook and Campbell, 1979, pp. 209–214).

Third, the interrupted time-series design allows for a more realistic analysis of social program impact than is permitted by designs that treat an effect as an observable event occurring at a single point in time after a program has been implemented. Glass, Willson, and Gottman (1975) note the unique perspective offered by the time-series design and how this perspective offers rich insight into the impact of social program or technology intervention.

> Interventions into societies and institutions do not have merely "an effect" but "an effect pattern" across time. The value of an intervention

is properly judged not by whether the effect is observable at the fall
harvest, but by whether the effect occurs immediately or is delayed,
whether it increases or decays, whether it is only temporarily or constantly superior to the effects of alternative interventions. The time-
series design provides a methodology appropriate to the complexity of
the effects of interventions into social organizations or with human
beings.

Finally, statistical procedures and software packages for analyzing the complexity of effect patterns have been developed that allow policy analysts and
program evaluators to move beyond visual scanning of data to reach conclusions
about hypothesized impacts. For example, Box and Jenkins (1970) have developed models and associated statistical techniques that allow applied researchers
to control for seasonal patterns and to analyze effect patterns considerably more
complex than abrupt, constant change (also see Pfeifer and Deutsch, 1980).
Further, McCain and McCleary (1979), and McCleary and Hay (1980) have
created a practical guide to give readers an understanding of the basic concept
surrounding the analysis of time-series data, and a few advanced texts on the
topic are available (Glass, Willson and Gottman, 1975; Box and Jenkins, 1970).
For a policy analyst or program evaluator only interested in obtaining the results
of these statistical procedures, computer programs are available for analyzing
interrupted, time-series data that estimate and test intervention effects (for
example, Bower, Padia, and Glass, 1974).

An Unsolved Problem: Designating Intervention

Despite the increasing sophistication of the interrupted time-series design,
this methodology is in a relatively early stage of development for applied research. As a developing technology, it still has a number of hurdles to clear,
among which is the lack of "construct validity of cause" surrounding the designation of the intervention point. Although Cook and Campbell (1979, p. 207)
argue that construct validity of cause or the fitting of cause operations to
their referent constructs is of low priority for many applied researchers, they
explicitly acknowledge the importance of designating the intervention point
that is the construct referent for cause associated with this design. Though they
acknowledge that this is often a complex issue, they offer little systematic advice
for attacking the problem. Specifically, they indicate that a researcher should
look for the *onset* of the treatment rather than its *widespread availability* in
choosing the intervention point (Cook and Campbell, 1979, p. 227).

But, what does *onset* mean? In their example of the British breathalyser
test, their designation of the intervention point did include a consideration of
whether the street-level bureaucrats (police officers) were prepared to use the
social technology associated with the "crackdown" (the breathalyser test), as

well as a consideration of whether citizens had been formally notified of the new policy (1979, p. 227). Despite Cook and Campbell's choice of *onset* over *widespread availability* to describe selection of the intervention point, they did take into account implementation of the policy in choosing the intervention point. However, as with most examples they use in their text, implementation lag is not a problem in the breathalyser study because "the time of onset was close to the time when most people would have a chance to be affected by the treatment" (1979, p. 226).

It is my contention that *implementation,* or assessing when the bureaucratic process has reached a point where targeted populations have a chance to be affected by the treatment (Nakamura and Smallwood, 1980, p. 1), must be included in the designation of the intervention point for applied research. Most applied researchers using the interrupted time-series design to study the impact of criminal justice policies assume onset to simply mean the point at which the policy was formally adopted. Such a legalistic interpretation of intervention allows for no consideration of its availability to the target population that is often delayed by the implementation process.

By rejecting widespread availability as a rule for choosing intervention points, Cook and Campbell apparently were warning against designating the intervention point after the social technology or program associated with the policy was widely diffused to the target population (1979, pp. 226-227). I distinguish between *organizational diffusion* and *target-group diffusion* to make clear two different problems related to the interrupted time-series design. Organizational diffusion is the process of implementing a public policy, and for this process, the researchers is interested in determining if (and when) a policy's treatment has been made widely available to the target population. Target-group diffusion refers to the nature and extent of the target population's exposure to the treatment. Transfer functions provide a number of options to control for variations in target-group diffusion (see, for example, McCain and McCleary, 1979, pp. 235-269).

However, organizational diffusion or *delayed causation* is not redressed by the use of transfer functions. This problem is partly a theoretical one that requires us to strengthen the construct validity of intervention to assure that implementation as well as adoption of a policy is considered in the designation of an intervention point. Failure to do so can lead to type-1 and type-2 errors.

The greatest threat is when a researcher designates an intervention to have occurred prior to implementation and then, analyzing outcome data, prematurely concludes that the policy is ineffective. Patton (1979, pp. 318-319) presents an exaggerated case of such a potential error in which a research team used a one-group pretest-posttest design. After a state legislature had adopted a demonstration program to teach welfare recipients the basic rudiments of parenting and household management, applied researchers selected and interviewed a sample of welfare recipients before and after the program was formally adopted. They concluded that the program was ineffective, but Patton (1979, p. 319) investigated further and found:

> As it turned out, there is a very good reason why the program was ineffective. When the funds were initially allocated from the state to the city, the program became immediately embroiled in the politics of urban welfare. Welfare rights organizations questioned the right of government to tell poor people how to spend their money or rear their children.
>
> As a result of these and other political battles the program was delayed and further delayed. Procrastination being the better part of valor, the first parenting brochure was never printed, no household management films were ever shown, no workshops were held, and no case workers were ever trained. In short, *the program was never implemented—but it was evaluated.*

Researchers using interrupted time-series designs to study the impacts of mandated policies and programs have used one of two basic approaches. The first, which can be called the *classical approach,* requires that the researcher designate the intervention point prior to any empirical analysis (Cook and Campbell, 1979, pp. 207–232). Here, researchers may be reaching incorrect conclusions because most studies rely on policy adoption dates to designate intervention points. Studies of complex policies that require considerable organizational implementation have designated intervention to be coterminous with adoption, including Zimring's 1975 analysis of the 1968 federal Gun-Control Act; Ross's 1975 study of Scandinavian drinking and driving laws; Ross, Campbell, and Glass's 1970 investigation of the British Road Safety Act; and Schnelle and Lees's 1974 investigation of the Tennessee State Prison's inmate transfer policy. Although in some cases the authors explicitly concluded that the treatment related to the policy was available to the target population on the date of adoption, others gave no consideration to implementation lag in arriving at an intervention point.

An example from my own use of the interrupted time-series design reveals more explicitly the potential for error associated with the classical approach. Aaronson, Dienes, and Musheno (1978) were interested in determining how laws that decriminalize public drunkenness, but continue to use the police as the intake agent, impact on police pickup rates. Because we assumed that decriminalization introduces many disincentives to police intervention using legally sanctioned procedures, we hypothesized that such laws would be followed by a statistically significant decline in the number of public inebriates formally handled by the police in a manner designated by the "law in the books" (1978, p. 415).

To test this hypothesis, we collected monthly rates of arrest for public drunkenness (predecriminalization) and of police deliveries to detoxification (detox) facilities (postdecriminalization) for two cities, Washington, D.C. (a high-arrest jurisdiction) and Minneapolis (a moderate-arrest jurisdiction). But, how did we arrive at designating the point of intervention in these cities? Before declaring the intervention point as required with the classical approach, we conducted a study of the policy formulation and implementation processes relevant to decriminalization in each jurisdiction (1978, pp. 407–415). For each city, we found three types of events relevant to this policy and its social program intervention: judicial rulings eliminating the use of the criminal sanction for public drunkenness; legislative mandates formally adopting decriminalization; and administrative appropriations for the construction, staffing, and opening of detoxification centers.

For Washington, D.C. (see figure 7-1), each event was discrete and sequential, with the administrative opening of the facility (I_3) taking place two years after the judicial ruling (I_1) and three months after the enabling legislation (I_2). For Minneapolis (see figure 7-2) the opening of the detox facility coincided with a legislative act that definitely embraced decriminalization (I_3); but, an earlier court ruling (I_1) and a legislative act (I_2) bearing significantly on decriminalization were adopted over four years prior to I_3.

Certainly, we could not assess the impact of decriminalization on police behavior until street officers *were notified about the new law by their superiors and had a facility available to them for delivering public inebriates*. In fact, if we had designated the intervention point to coincide with I_1 in Washington, D.C., or either I_1 or I_2 in Minneapolis (all events associated with formal adoption), our analysis would have led us to accept the null hypothesis when in fact it was false. Police intake rates significantly declined only when implementation lag was built into the designation of the intervention point (1978, pp. 419–420).

Another group of researchers have recently proposed an *inductive, empirical approach* for designating intervention points relevant to the interrupted time-series analysis of mandate policies (Deutsch and Alt, 1977).[2] In analyzing the impact of the Massachusetts Gun Control Law, Deutsch and Alt identify an initial reference point in time prior to the adoption of the legislation (N_1) and using auto regressive integrated moving average methods (Box and Jenkins, 1970), they investigate whether crime rates associated with points in time one, two, three, or four months after N_1 (designated as N_2) reveal "a statistically significant process shift" (p. 561). When no significant shift in level is discovered using the initial reference point, N_1 is redesignated as a later date and they again sequentially update N_2 as just described.

Such an empirical approach does allow an analyst to find an intervention point relevant to a broad time framework associated with the mandate under study which produces a dramatic shift in level. However, with this technique, the problem becomes one of determining whether the point of intervention is reliably associated with an event relevant to the implementation of the policy under study or is attributable to some unrelated event.

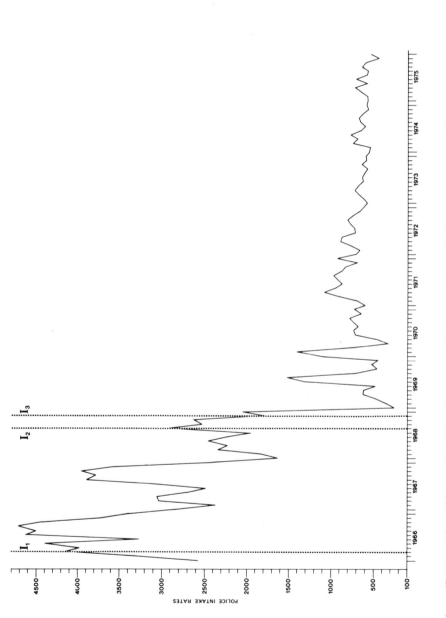

Source: Based on official statistics of Metropolitan Police Department, Washington, D.C., and official records of the D.C. Detoxification Center.

Figure 7-1 Monthly Police Intake Rates for Public Intoxication: Washington, D.C.

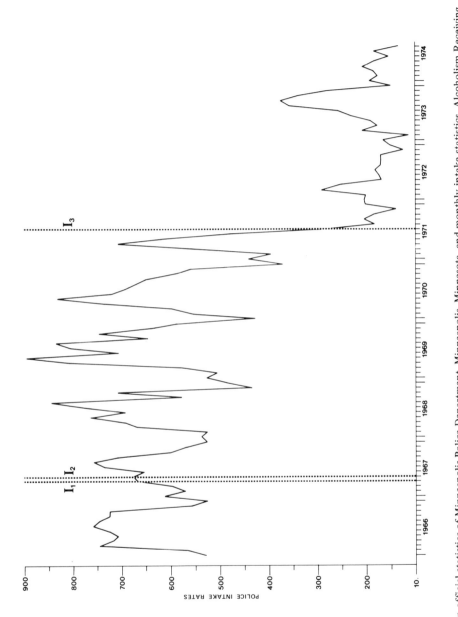

Source: Based on official statistics of Minneapolis Police Department, Minneapolis, Minnesota, and monthly intake statistics, Alcoholism Receiving Center.

Figure 7-2. Monthly Police Intake Rates for Public Intoxication: Minneapolis, Minnesota

In short, whether a policy analyst uses the classical or the inductive approach, he must face the construct validity problem identified here. He can choose to face the problem earlier (prior to analysis) or later (once the analysis is completed); but either way, improving the construct validity of cause associated with intervention is essential to interrupted time-series analysis of mandate policies.

Resolving the Problem: A Theoretical Approach

To improve construct validity, one must take a theoretical approach to the problem, working toward a set of decision rules concerning the identification of intervention points. Two bodies of literature seem potentially valuable for initiating a macrosolution.

Implementation Studies

The literature on policy implementation is rapidly developing (see Pressman and Wildavsky, 1973; Bardach, 1977; Williams and Elmore, 1976; Prottas, 1979; Nakamura and Smallwood, 1980). A number of scholars in this area have identified constructs for: (1) distinguishing types of policy; (2) classifying *intermediaries* and *communication linkages* relevant to legislative versus judicial implementation; (3) identifying factors relevant to implementation failure; and (4) differentiating processes associated with micro- and macro-implementation.

For example, Montjoy and O'Toole (1979) identify different types of policy mandates according to their specificity and the amount of resources that accompany them. They argue that policies that are specific (that is, governed by specific external directives) and that provide new resources are likely to experience straightforward implementation. By applying their model to a particular policy area (such as criminal justice), a policy analyst might be able to develop guidelines and identify relevant resource data to track the extent of implementation lag.

Nakamura and Smallwood assert that one can classify *intermediaries* or "groups that are delegated responsibility by formal implementers to assist in carrying out public policies "for mandates adopted by legislatures and similarly for judicial mandates (1980, pp. 47, 84-107). They also identify alternative *implementation linkages* or communication patterns necessary to hold the implementation process together (pp. 114-115). Again, for a particular policy area, decision rules and qualitative research methods could be identified for determining if and when intermediaries acted and communication patterns were linked.[3] The development of decision rules tied to qualitative data-collection techniques also seems appropriate for checking whether implementation failure has occurred for a class of public policies (see Larson, 1980, pp. 1-16).

Berman (1978) distinguishes *macroimplementation* from *microimplementation* to indicate the differences in the institutional settings of federal and local systems. For each type of implementation setting, he tentatively identifies phases that policies generally go through before they are institutionalized. Using such studies, one might develop indicators and output data from various phases of implementation relevant to a policy area that time series analysts can look for in arriving at the designation of an intervention point.

Innovation Research

Another potentially helpful body of literature is the writing on innovations, particularly technological innovations (see Zaltman, Duncan, and Holbek, 1973; Bingham, 1976; Radner et al., 1978; Lambright, 1979; Perry and Kraemer, 1980). Here, researchers offer insights for reducing analysis of *public policy* to its researchable components, and suggest a series of stages associated with the implementation of technologies.

As mentioned earlier, one can identify technologies and programs associated with a particular policy. These distinctions might help time-series analysts break crime policies or housing policies into more finite components for assessing implementation lag. For example, it is likely that social technologies based on considerable scientific development are less susceptible to manipulation by bureaucracies than social programs that have yet to be clearly defined.

In studying the diffusion of technological innovations, Rogers (1978) has tentatively identified a number of different stages than an invention must go through before it is interconnected or integrated into its organizational setting. A group of policy analysts are currently applying Rogers's model to the study of social-program technologies (see Lambright, 1980). If these stages of the innovation process can be used to study the implementation of social-program technologies, time-series analysts may be able to use a checklist of stages and output data associated with these stages to determine whether or not components of a policy they want to investigate have been organizationally diffused or implemented.

Research Strategy

In that policy researchers, including those using interrupted time-series analysis to assess impact, identify themselves with policy areas (such as crime policy or social-welfare policy), decision rules relevant to intervention should be developed along these lines. Although rules need to include both similarities and differences between legislative and judicial implementation processes, many policies, like decriminalization of public drunkenness, are implemented as a result of a combination of judicial and legislative actions.

According to the literature on interrupted time-series analysis policy implementation and innovation research are fitted to a particular policy area, and
researchers: (1) refine the operational definition of *intervention* as it applies to
the interrupted time-series analysis of a class of policies; and (2) present a
tentative set of decision rules to guide applied researchers using the interrupted
time-series design to study the impacts of such policies.

These decision rules would be exposed to a panel of policy and time-series
experts to assure high construct validity in refining the operational definition,
proposing a set of decision rules, and fitting the rules to the analytic techniques
just described. A second panel would be given a full write-up and data relevant
to actual policy innovations and asked to designate the proper intervention
points using the tentative decision rules.

If some of the policy innovations were drawn from interrupted time-series
studies already completed, the final assessment of the construct validity of
policy intervention would allow checks on the consistency in interpreting the
rules, and checks on whether following the rules produces outcomes significantly
different from findings reached without the benefit of the rules.

Conclusion: Ameliorating the Problem

Short of such an undertaking, how can applied researchers immediately assure
that implementation lag or delayed causation is taken into account in designating
intervention points for the interrupted time-series design? A number of policy
analysts are urging applied researchers to study both the implementation and
impact of policies under scrutiny (see Elmore, 1978, pp. 186-187). However,
conducting a thorough process and impact analysis of a particular public policy
requires extensive site visitation and significant fiscal resources to sustain such
a comprehensive study. Although such efforts are desirable, applied researchers
have no literature that provides them with guidelines for collecting qualitative
and quantitative data related to implementation where at least part of their
purpose is to arrive at the selection of an intervention point.

Alternatively, researchers could use convergent methods, designating and
analyzing policy interventions as suggested with the classical approach, and also
searching for the intervention point through dynamic intervention analysis as
suggested with the inductive empirical method. By cross-checking findings,
researchers could be much more confident in their assessment of policy impact.

Other potential avenues for resolving problems associated with the designation of the intervention point, which are largely individualistic and limited in
application, include relying on crude time intervals (such as years) over more
precise ones (such as months or weeks) in the time-series; employing more
sophisticated time-series designs, including the *switching replications* design
(Cook and Campbell, 1979, pp. 224-225); and checking critical output data to

make sure significant implementation activity of key policy intermediaries (such as street-level bureaucrats) is being registered before designating intervention. Regarding this latter strategy, if one were interested in determining whether the health conditions of public inebriates were improved under decriminalization, one could use police and other intake data (as described earlier) to initially determine whether inebriates were being delivered to public health facilities, or alternatively, being left on the streets at a higher rate after decriminalization. If critical intake agents were ignoring the requirements of the policy, time-series analysis of inebriates' health conditions would be inappropriate.

Although any one or a combination of these approaches for determining when an intervention occurred might be useful for a particular study, they do not represent strategies for improving our general understanding of policy intervention. Therefore, they are unlikely to improve our ability to determine intervention policies in time-series analysis.

Notes

1. New ideas or inventions in the public sector can be categorized as material technologies, social technologies, or social programs. Although these are not discrete categories, one can generally distinguish those inventions in the public sector which have their roots and development closely linked to rigorous scientific research and hypothesis testing (that is, material and social technologies) versus those shifts in organizational strategies adopted and developed largely through political incentives (social programs) such as demonstration grants awarded by the federal bureaucracy to local governments (see Tornatsky et al., 1979; Lambright, 1979, pp. 71-72.

2. Individuals associated with the classical approach and those associated with the empirical approach have engaged in intellectual warfare with one another (see Hay and McCleary, 1979; Deutsch, 1979).

3. Efforts are currently under way to identify and refine qualitative methods for studying policy implementation (see, for example, Jick, 1979; Pettigrew, 1979, pp. 571-574).

References

Aaronson, D.E.; Dienes, C.T., and Musheno, M.C. "Changing the Public Drunkenness Laws: The Impact of Decriminalization." *Law and Society Review* 12 (1978): 405-436.

Bardach, E. *The Implementation Game.* Cambridge, Mass.: MIT Press, 1977.

Berman, Paul. "The Study of Macro- and Micro-Implementation." *Public Policy* 20 (1978): 157-184.

Bingham, R.D. *The Adoption of Innovations in Local Government*. Lexington, Mass.: Lexington Books, D.C. Heath and Company, 1976.

Bower, C.P.; Padia, W.L., and Glass, G.V. *Two Fortran 4 Programs for Analysis of Time Series Experiments*. Boulder, Colorado: Laboratory of Educational Research, University of Colorado, 1974.

Box, G.E.P., and Jenkins, G.M. *Time-Series Analysis: Forecasting and Control*. San Francisco: Holden Day, 1970.

Campbell, D.T. "Reforms as Experiments." *American Psychologist* 24 (1969): 409-429.

Campbell, D.T., and Stanley, J.C. *Experimental and Quasi-Experimental Designs for Research*. Chicago: Rand McNally, 1963.

Cook, T.D., and Campbell, D.T. *Quasi-Experimentation: Design and Analysis Issues for Field Settings*. Chicago: Rand McNally, 1979.

Deutsch, Stuart. "Lies, Damn Lies, and Statistics." *Evaluation Quarterly* 3 (1979): 315-328.

Deutsch, S.J., and Alt, F.B. "The Effect of Massachusetts' Gun Control Law on Gun-Related Crimes in the City of Boston." *Evaluation Quarterly* 1 (1977): 543-568.

Elmore, Richard. "Organizational Models of Social Program Implementation." *Public Policy* 26 (1978): 185-228.

Glass, G.V.; Willson, V.L.; and Gottman, J.M. *Design and Analysis of Time-Series Experiments*. Boulder, Colorado: Colorado Associated University Press, 1975.

Hay, Richard A., and McCleary, Richard. "Box-Tiao Time Series Models for Impact Assessment." *Evaluation Quarterly* 3 (1979): 277-314.

Jick, Todd. "Mixing Qualitative and Quantitative Methods," *Administrative Science Quarterly* 24 (1979): 602-612.

Lambright, W. Henry. *Technology Transfer to Cities: Process of Choice at the Local Level*. Boulder, Colorado: Westview, 1979.

Larson, James. *Why Government Programs Fail*. New York; Praeger, 1980.

Lempert, Richard. "Strategies of Research Design in the Legal Impact Study." *Law and Society Review* 1 (1966): 111-132.

Levine, J.P.; Musheno, M.C.; and Palumbo, D.J. *Criminal Justice: A Public Policy Approach*. New York: Harcourt Brace Jovanovich, 1980.

McCain, L.J., and McCleary, R. "The Statistical Analysis of the Simple Interrupted Time-Series Quasi-Experiment." In *Quasi-Experimentation*, edited by T.D. Cook and D.T. Campbell, pp. 233-293. Chicago: Rand McNally, 1979.

McCleary, R., and Hay, R.A., Jr. *Applied Time-Series Analysis for the Social Sciences*. Beverly Hills, Calif.: Sage Publications, 1980.

Montjoy, R.S., and O'Toole, L.J. "Toward a Theory of Policy Implementation: An Organizational Perspective." *Public Administration Review* 39 (1979): 465-476.

Nakamura, Robert, and Frank Smallwood. *The Politics of Policy Implementation.* New York: St. Martin's Press, 1980.

Patton, Michael Quinn. "Evaluation of Program Implementation." In *Evaluation of Studies Review Annual. Vol. 4,* edited by L. Sechrest et al., pp. 318-346. Beverly Hills, Calif.: Sage Publications, 1979.

Perry, James, and Kraemer, Kenneth. *Technological Innovation in American Local Governments.* New York: Pergamon, 1980.

Pettigrew, Andrew. "On Studying Organizational Cultures." In *Qualitative and Quantitative Methods in Evaluation Research,* edited by Charles Reichardt and Thomas Cook. Beverly Hills, Calif.: Sage Publications, 1979.

Pfeifer, Phillip E., and Deutsch, Stuart J. "A Three-Stage Iterative Procedure for Space-Time Modeling." *Technometrics* 22 (1980): 35-47.

Pressman, J.L., and Wildavsky, A.B. *Implementation.* Berkeley, Calif.: University of California Press, 1973.

Prottas, Jeffrey. *People Processing.* Lexington, Mass.: Lexington Books, D.C. Heath and Company, 1979.

Radner, M. et al., eds. *The Diffusion of Innovations: An Assessment.* Evanston, Ill.: Northwestern University, 1978.

Rogers, Everett. "Re-Invention during the Innovation Process." In *The Diffusion of Innovations: An Assessment,* edited by M. Radner et al. Evanston, Ill.: Northwestern University, 1978.

Ross, H.L. "The Scandinavian Myth: The Effectiveness of Drinking-and-Driving Legislation in Sweden and Norway." *Journal of Legal Studies* 4 (1975): 285-310.

Ross, H.L., Campbell, D.T., and Glass, G.V. "Determining the Social Effects of a Legal Reform: The British 'Breathalyser' Crackdown of 1967." *American Behavioral Scientists* 13 (1970): 493-509.

Schnelle, J.F., and Lees, J.F. "A Quasi-Experimental Retrospective Evaluation of a Prison Policy Change." *Journal of Applied Behavioral Analysis* 7 (1974): 422-444.

Tornatsky, L. et al. *Bibliographic Essay on Innovation Research.* Washington, D.C.: National Science Foundation, 1979.

Williams, W., and Elmore, R.F. eds. *Social Program Implementation.* New York: John Wiley, 1976.

Zaltman, G.; Duncan, R.; and Holbek, J. *Innovations and Organizations.* New York: John Wiley, 1973.

Zimring, F. "Firearms and Federal Law: The Gun Control Act of 1968." *Journal of Legal Studies* 4 (1975): 133-198.

8

"Patching Up" Evaluation Designs: The Case for Process Evaluation

John Clayton Thomas

Many questions have been raised about outcome evaluation techniques for public programs since those techniques came into vogue in the 1960s. The most serious of these have concerned the validity of the findings that come from outcome evaluations and the utility of those findings, if valid, for governmental decision makers. Those questions have led some critics (for example, Weiss and Rein, 1970) to suggest that outcome evaluations be abandoned for many or most public programs, and others (such as Floden and Weiner, 1978) to suggest that they be retained, but with their functions radically redefined.

I take a considerably different point of view. Although accepting many of the criticisms of outcome evaluation techniques as valid, I hold that those criticisms can be dealt with in part by more widespread use of process evaluation techniques. Evaluation research has tended to be concerned with the relationship of inputs to outcomes, but with little attention given to the role of program process in linking inputs to outcomes. Process evaluation techniques, I will argue (using examples from an evaluation of a municipal government affirmative-action program), can be used to "patch up" (Weiss, 1972, p. 72) the holes that are perhaps inherent in the fabric of outcome evaluation techniques. In so doing, we may make evaluation techniques better tools in our effort to optimize the achievement of policy goals.

Definition: Forms of Evaluation

The first task must be to define the different forms of evaluation, as well as the distinction between *outcome evaluation techniques* and *process evaluation techniques*. Outcome evaluation techniques include any techniques that (1) focus on measurable program outcomes and (2) have some controls or comparisons to deal with alternative explanations of changes in those outcomes.

The purest examples are experimental evaluation designs that attempt to assess the effect of a treatment (that is, program) on a measurable outcome in a tightly controlled situation. The so-called quasi-experimental designs (see Campbell, 1972) also belong with these techniques. The category might even encompass the most primitive preexperimental designs (Clark, 1977) because they do focus on measurable outcomes and have at least some, albeit inadequate, controls. They can be included because there is no stamp of approval implied in the designation, *outcome evaluation technique.* In fact, the argument here is that, no matter how rigorous the outcome evaluation, it can probably be improved by use of process evaluation techniques.

Process evaluation is an umbrella term for a variety of techniques that can be used to evaluate program process and its contribution to the achievement of program goals. These techniques have in common the concern with program process as contrasted to the outcome evaluation's often exclusive concern with outcomes. Pressman and Wildavsky (1973, p. xiv) suggested that a policy is an *if-then* statement: if *x* is done, then *y* will result. In this context, process evaluation examines the extent to which *x*, the *if*, has occurred, and, perhaps, how that occurrence has contributed to the achievement of program goals. Also, process evaluation techniques are likely to lack controls. They can be viewed as substituting case-study detail for the comparative and experimental rigor of outcome evaluations.

Process evaluation has recently become a major concern of policy analysts and evaluators. Unfortunately, the increased concern has been accompanied by a proliferation of terms for what might be included within the concept of process evaluation. It appears, however, that the terms can be reduced to two major aspects or techniques of process evaluation: (1) implementation assessment, and (2) performance monitoring.

Implementation assessment is a term used by Williams (1975, pp. 532-34) to refer to analyses of program process at several stages of program development and operation. The term is used here to refer only to Williams's *final implementation assessment,* the assessment of "the degree to which a field activity corresponds to its design specifications" to determine whether the "field activity is fully operational."

Implementation assessment is an essentially qualitative process, where *performance monitoring* is more quantitative. If policy implementation is viewed as a chain of steps, implementation assessment examines whether each of the links in the chain has been completed. The chain simile is imperfect, however, because implementation assessment also involves examining how the actual program varies from the anticipated program, in what has been referred to as *discrepancy evaluation* (Provus, 1971).

To the extent possible, implementation assessment should go beyond these descriptive tasks to the analytical task of explaining any discrepancies between the expected and the actual program. Of particular interest is whether those discrepancies are based on (1) chance or accidental factors, (2) contextual factors (factors in the context of the locale of implementation), or (3) factors integral to the program. Implementation discrepancies based on chance factors may suggest that another implementation of the program would be unlikely to encounter the same problem. Discrepancies based on contextual factors suggest that the program is unlikely to be successfully implemented in the current locale, but perhaps could be successfully implemented elsewhere. Finally, discrepancies based on factors integral to the program would suggest difficulties in the program itself.

By way of illustration, the implementation of Cincinnati's affirmative-action program was delayed—and the program's impact consequently reduced—when the program's director died in office.[1] This is perhaps the clearest example of a chance factor, one that would be unlikely to recur in other implementations of the program. On the other hand, the program's implementation had also been delayed by the resignation of an earlier program director. Although this, too, could have been a chance factor, it might instead have been a contextual factor since that director was known to be dissatisfied with the city's progress in accepting affirmative action. Thus, distinguishing the reasons for implementation problems is not easy, but it is worth the effort.

The other side of process evaluation is performance monitoring, by which is meant the monitoring of the level of program activities (see Altman, 1979). Performance monitoring is premised on some degree of successful implementation; that is, the program as operating can be viewed as sufficiently close to the intended program that efforts can proceed to examine program results.

Although performance monitoring is sometimes defined to encompass monitoring of achievement of program goals, the emphasis here is on activity levels—program *outputs* as opposed to *outcomes* (although the relationship of the two should be examined whenever possible). In affirmative-action recruitment efforts, the ouput-outcome distinction corresponds to the difference between level of recruitment efforts (for example, number of minority organizations visited, amount of advertising in minority media) and numbers of minorities actually recruited and hired. The distinction cannot be made with every program. A highway maintenance program, for example, may have the number of streets repaved (or potholes filled) as both the employee activity level and the program's outcome goal. Only close examination can reveal whether the distinction can be made with a particular program.

Since performance monitoring examines activity *levels*, it can usually be quantitative. In affirmative-action efforts focused on employee-selection techniques, for example, performance monitoring reports such data as the number of civil-service examinations reviewed and revised and number of changes in minimum requirements.[2]

One danger in making this effort is the possibility of being overwhelmed by data. This danger can be minimized if the evaluator plans beforehand to collect data only at key junctures in the program where activity levels can be measured, rather than succumbing to the temptation to collect data wherever data are available.

The definition of these process evaluation techniques could usefully be given more attention. However, the prior task—and the primary purpose of this chapter—is to explain the underlying rationale for the use of process evaluation techniques. We must, in other words, explain *why* process should be examined before we consider in any detail *how* it should be examined.

The Argument for Process Evaluation

Outcome evaluation techniques have been criticized for having a variety of problems. The case for process evaluation rests on its potential for dealing with some of these problems, principally those pertaining to the frequent lack of controls in public programs and to the often limited utility of the information provided by outcome evaluations.

Problems with Controls

The idea behind outcome evaluations is that controls over influences external to the program are so extensive that any changes in outcome measures can be interpreted as reflecting program effects. The controls rule out any possibility that the changes could be based on other influences.

The problem is that controls this extensive can seldom, if ever, be attained in actual public programs. This fact severely limits the applicability of outcome evaluation techniques to public programs. This problem has been mitigated by using quasi-experimental designs where longitudinal measurements and ad hoc comparisons compensate for the lack of controls and tests for the role of factors that are not experimentally controlled, that is, "plausible rival alternative hypothese" (see Webb, Campbell, and Schwartz, 1966).

These approaches cannot solve the problem of limited controls, but they can reduce it. Process evaluation techniques can further reduce the problem. They can do so through their emphasis on *close causation*, that is, an examination of each program step in the hypothesized process of program cause and effect. Outcome evaluation techniques disdain examination of this process because controls are so extensive that there is no need to know what happens in the unseen "black box" of actual program operation. If controls are not that extensive—and they usually are not—perhaps their absence can be partially compensated for by an analysis of what happened in the black box.

This is termed a *close causation* approach because the cause-effect linkages being examined are relatively close to each other, in contrast to the frequent outcome evaluation focus on a single, relatively long cause-effect linkage of program inputs to outcomes. The idea is to examine each of the steps in the program's planned implementation and the activity levels at each of the program's major junctures. These examinations should, at a minimum, offer some clues on whether the program became enough of a reality to have possibly produced any of the intended outcomes.

Close causation, to be sure, lacks controls, a fact that casts doubt on any causal statements that might result from using the approach. However, the findings of the approach are not intended to stand on their own; they are to be considered in combination with the findings of whatever outcome evaluation is possible on the same program.

The value of the approach becomes more evident when viewed relative to particular control problems, in this case problems that arose in an attempt to evaluate an affirmative-action program. That program was an excellent example of a program lacking in controls over outside influences. In particular, how could any control be placed on the role of the civil rights movement generally as opposed to affirmative action specifically, in prompting minority employment increases in Cincinnati? That is what Campbell (1972, p. 192) has referred to as *multiple treatment interference*. A partial solution might be to use another city government—one comparable in most ways to Cincinnati, but lacking an affirmative-action program—as a comparison city in a quasi-experimental design. However, the nature of federal affirmative-action requirements means that any city comparable to Cincinnati in most ways is also likely to be comparable in the development of an affirmative-action program.

The program was evaluated, instead, with a time-series design supplemented by the two kinds of process evaluation, and the use of the latter did permit at least an educated guess on the relative influences of affirmative action as opposed to the civil rights movement generally on the city's minority employment. Examination of the processes behind increases in the city's employment of minorities revealed that the increase resulted from city actions occurring prior to—and apparently independent of—the federal push for the city adoption of an affirmative-action program. The most significant increases had come in the police and fire services, and those increases could be traced to a process of stepped-up recruitment efforts beginning in the early to middle 1960s, well before the city's adoption of affirmative action. Thus, the affirmative-action program could not be credited with the minority employment improvements.

Another common control problem is that programs tend to be put into operation only gradually; yet as Campbell (1972) has noted, a program should be instituted as an abrupt change if our usually imprecise outcome measures are going to reflect any program effect. Cincinnati's affirmative-action program again is a good example. It was preceded by various piecemeal efforts to increase minority employment, efforts making the actual affirmative-action program only an incremental change; and, the program itself was put into operation only slowly, as suggested by the turnover in program directors noted earlier. This made virtually impossible any assessment of program effects through an outcome evaluation alone. However, examination of the program's process made possible some judgments on the role of the program in creating the outcome measure changes.

The Nonutilization Problem

Most evaluation research is applied research: its purpose is to provide information that decision makers will utilize in planning public programs. Yet, most evidence (see Goldstein, Marcus, and Rausch, 1978; Patton, 1978) suggests that outcome evaluations have proved to be of limited use for decision makers. The use of process evaluation techniques can increase the potential for utilization of evaluation research findings, as can be seen by examining some of the specifics of the nonutilization problem.

One problem concerns the limited information that outcome evaluations can provide (Weiss and Rein, 1970, p. 103), information indicating the extent of program success or failure, but not the reasons for that success or failure. Although that information can be valuable for a decision on whether to continue or terminate a program, most decisions are not of that kind. In a world of incremental change, decisions are much more likely to concern how programs can be marginally modified to increase effectiveness. With the Cincinnati affirmative-action program, for example, federal grant requirements and local political realities dictated that the program would continue, but not the precise form in which it would continue. On the latter issue, a process evaluation can be valuable by indicating the role of different program components in overall program effectiveness.

Another aspect of the nonutilization problem is the frequently *counter-intuitive* nature of evaluation findings (Caplan, 1976, p. 232), findings that often indicate no effects for programs that staff and clients may perceive as effective. Findings of no program effect might be made intuitively more appealing if they were explained in terms of program process, as is possible when an outcome evaluation is supplemented by process evaluation. Realistically, nothing is likely to make such findings attractive to program staff, but a better explanation of the findings might at least decrease the resistance to them and so make their utilization more likely. In addition, the analysis of program process might reveal modest program effects not suggested by the outcome evaluation.

Lack of Outcome Measures

A third problem with outcome evaluation techniques is the frequent lack of satisfactory outcome measures. In some cases, as with many law-enforcement programs, *instrumentation* (Campbell, 1972, p. 197-198) changes when the program begins, and the result is an uninterpretable pre- to post-program difference in the outcome measure. In other cases, as often with health programs, the outcome goals are too broad or diffuse for any particular aggregate measures to be likely to reflect program impacts.

This problem is an especially vexing one because it undermines the potential for using any kind of outcome evaluation technique. Process evaluation techniques cannot compensate for the lack of outcome measures, but they can at least produce some evaluation where none would otherwise be possible. In other words, it is still valuable to know whether a program is producing the desired outputs, even if we cannot assess its effects in terms of intended outcomes.

Conclusions

Process evaluation is not a cure-all for what ails outcome evaluation techniques. The latter suffer from some problems that process evaluation techniques may not be able to remedy. With the difficulty of defining the goals of public programs, for example, process evaluation techniques can be employed in the hope that program goals, indistinct in policy statements, will become distinct in actual program operation. However, contrary to what Weiss and Rein (1970) argue, if the goals do not become evident at some point, it is difficult to see how the program can be evaluated in anything other than a kind of pork-barrel counting of hands for and against.

Otherwise, process evaluation techniques should be applicable to almost any program where an outcome evaluation is possible. Cost considerations should place only modest limits on their applicability. Implementation assessments should be possible in any program, since documenting the degree to which a program has been put into operation is unlikely to be either costly or time consuming. Performance monitoring could be more costly, but these costs could be minimized if program staff, as part of their duties, were maintaining records of activity levels at key program junctures.

The most important caution to offer on process evaluation is that it cannot be a substitute for outcome evaluation (even in those cases where a process evaluation is possible, but an outcome evaluation is not). Evaluations once tended to overlook outcomes in favor of process; program staff felt much more secure reporting what they did than attempting to discern what those efforts achieved. The disdain of outcome evaluators for program process may be in part a reaction against this earlier emphasis on process. We should be careful that our renewed concern with program process does not result in a regression to that earlier emphasis.

If used appropriately—that is, in combination with outcome evaluation techniques, process evaluation techniques can improve both the methodological rigor and the utilization potential of evaluation research findings. That improvement, in turn, should contribute to the broader sense of public policy "optimizing" to which this book is dedicated.

Notes

1. All affirmative-action examples in this chapter are taken from Thomas and Shocket, 1977.

2. For more on measurements, see Morris and Fitz-Gibbon, 1978.

References

Altman, S. "Performance Monitoring Systems for Public Managers." *Public Administration Review* 39 (January/February 1979):31-35.

Campbell, D.T. "Reforms as Experiments." In *Evaluating Action Programs: Readings in Social Action and Education,* edited by C.H. Weiss, pp. 187-223. Boston: Allyn and Bacon, 1972.

Caplan, N. "Factors Associated with Knowledge Use among Federal Executives." *Policy Studies Journal* 4 (Spring 1976):229-234.

Clark, L.P. *Designs for Evaluating Social Programs.* Croton-on-Hudson, N.Y.: Policy Studies Associates, 1977.

Floden, R.E., and Weiner, S.C. "Rationality to Ritual: The Multiple Roles of Evaluation in Governmental Processes." *Policy Sciences* 9 (February 1978):9-18.

Goldstein, M.S.; Marcus, A.C.; and Rausch, N.P. "The Nonutilization of Evaluation Research." *Pacific Sociological Review* 21 (January 1978):21-44.

Morris, L.L., and Fitz-Gibbon, C.T. *How to Measure Program Implementation.* Beverly Hills and London: Sage Publications, 1978.

Patton, M.Q. *Utilization-Focused Evaluation.* Beverly Hills and London: Sage Publications, 1978, pp. 165-167.

Pressman, J.L., and Wildavsky, A. *Implementation.* Berkeley: University of California Press, 1973, p. xiv.

Provus, M. *Discrepancy Evaluation for Educational Program Improvement and Assessment.* Berkeley: McCutchan, 1971.

Thomas, J.C., and Shocket, P.A. "The Politics of Non-implementation: The Failure of Federal Minority Employment Policies in Cincinnati." Paper prepared for annual meeting of Midwest Political Science Association, Chicago, Ill., 1977.

Webb, E.J.; Campbell, D.T.; Schwartz, R.D.; and Sechrest, L. *Unobtrusive Measures: Nonreactive Research in the Social Sciences.* Chicago: Rand McNally, 1966.

Weiss, C.H. *Evaluation Research.* Englewood Cliffs, N.J.: Prentice-Hall, 1972.

Weiss, R.S., and Rein, M. "The Evaluation of Broad-Aim Programs: Experimental Design, Its Difficulties, and an Alternative." *Administrative Science Quarterly* 15 (1970):97-109.

Williams, W. "Implementation Analysis and Assessment." *Policy Analysis* 1 (Summer 1975): pp. 531-566.

9 Models of Implementation and Policy Evaluation: Choice and Its Implications

Elaine B. Sharp

To a great extent, developments in implementation theory and in evaluation research are interlinked. Each field has served as a catalyst for the other. Evaluation research has stimulated implementation research because the apparent failures of the "massive social programs" of the 1960s (Berman, 1978) are often seen as being a result of implementation problems (Pressman and Wildavsky, 1973).

One purpose of this chapter is to show that there is a link between classic implementation models and the classic model of evaluation—a link that has directed recent implementation research toward viewing the policy process in terms of hierarchy, control/compliance, and centralized decision making.[1] This classic model of implementation has been called into question by recent research that documents adaptive processes in bureaucracies and the use of street-level discretion. In a parallel fashion, evaluation research has had to develop an alternative to its traditional, impact/experimental design-oriented model. The result of all these developments is that we now have competing models in both evaluation research and implementation research.

A second purpose of this chapter is to briefly describe the emergence of the more recent implementation model, and the parallel evaluation research model—each contrasting markedly with its respective classical counterpart.

A third section of the chapter focuses on the issue of choice between the two types of approaches. Because implementation and policy evaluation are so interdependent, policy evaluation based on a given model will point toward the concepts and values of the corresponding implementation model, and vice versa. Choice between the classic models and the revisionist models determines what we ask about a particular experience of policy implementation, and may have a bearing on our conclusions about the success of the policy and its implementation.

Classic Evaluation Research and Implementation
Theory: Paradigmatic Partners

The classic model of evaluation is one based on the paradigm of experimental design (Houston, 1972). This is not to say that evaluation researchers believe that all policy evaluation can meet all the requirements of the classic experimental design. It is to say, however, that policy evaluation is premised on the notion of an experimenting society, in which the rationality of policy decision is increased by systemmatic evidence on the extent to which implemented programs actually meet specifically stated goals (Weiss, 1972). Furthermore, the ideal of "systematic evidence" about the impact of policy on stated goals is found through experimental design.

When applied to public policy, experimental design requires (1) clearly specified goals; (2) conceiving policy as a standardized treatment directed at a specific target group or groups; and (3) a controlled setting.

One of the most common themes in the literature on evaluation research is the importance, and difficulty, of establishing clear goals (that is, criteria for success) in order to conduct the evaluation. It is recognized that policies frequently encompass vague, multiple, and sometimes contradictory goals, and that impact evaluation, which requires the comparison of measurable results with expected results, cannot proceed unless the goal specification issue is untangled. Unless it totally eschews the goal model, evaluation research must continually confront the need for somehow specifying, in advance of actual empirical work, what results, outcomes, or impacts are expected of the policy being evaluated. Hence, texts on evaluation research regularly stipulate goal specification as an initial step in the evaluation process, and present strategies for developing such goal statements (see, for example, Borus, 1979).

An important normative theme that emerges from this wrangle over goal specification is that it is preferable to have policies that embody clearly defined and ordered goals. Here, the linkage with implementation theory becomes evident. Many recent case studies of implementation failure suggest that confusion over goals is a significant part of the implementation problem (Bardach, 1977; Moynihan, 1970; Derthick, 1972). More important, recent attempts to develop comprehensive models of implementation have adopted this theme. An excellent example, and one that will be referred to with respect to later principles as well, is Sabatier and Mazmanian's (1979) analysis of the "conditions for effective implementation." One of their conditions directly parallels the evaluation research movement's call for goal specification, and in fact, acknowledges that this goal specification is of value not only for effective implementation but also for evaluation. They write (1979, p. 487) that "Statutory objectives that are precise and clearly ranked in importance serve as an indispensable aid in program evaluation, as unambiguous directives to implementing officials, and as a resource available to supporters of those objectives both inside and outside the implementing agencies."

The principle of precise, clearly ordered goals is closely linked to the conception of policy innovations as being based on a sound, deductive theory, and the corresponding experimental design principle that the experiment tests hypotheses logically derived from a theory. Pressman and Wildavsky (1973) were perhaps the first to point out to implementation researchers that policy does imply a theory—that if one does x, y should result. Berman (1978) has elaborated on this notion, pointing out that the theory being tested in any policy implementation situation actually has two components—the technical validity of the policy and the effectiveness of its implementation design. Sabatier and Mazmanian (1979, p. 486) use the terms *technical* and *compliance* to refer to these same two components, and include in their list of conditions for effective implementation the stipulation that "the program is based on a sound theory relating changes in target group behavior to the achievement of the desired end-state [objectives] ."

But what if there is no preexisting sound theory stipulating what specific structural and behavioral changes should lead to outcome Y? What if we encounter a policy that stipulates that an organization change its operations toward the purpose of a desired end-state Y, but does not stipulate the specific means to get there, because little is known about the causal linkages between behavioral change and the desired end-state? Sabatier and Mazmanian's discussion, and that of much classical implementation theory, implies that implementation is unlikely to succeed under such circumstances—that organizations need to be *directed* to specific means if desired ends are ever to be achieved. There is little room in this orientation for a "muddling through" approach to implementation, or the decentralized, trial-and-error approach that has characterized many attempts at policy implementation. It is, rather, much more amenable to a centralized, directive model of organizational change.

The second element of the experimental-design paradigm that has had an impact on implementation theory is the notion of experimental intervention as a standardized "treatment" variable, directed toward a predefined target group.

The notions of a treatment and a target group are crucial to the experimental design for obvious reasons. If we cannot designate which individuals a policy is to affect, we cannot evaluate the policy any more than we could without knowing what effects it is meant to have. Furthermore, to insure that the policy or program being evaluated, and not some confounding factor, is responsible for whatever observed effects the experiment shows, we must be able to control, or at least know, who is exposed to the policy treatment and when. Finally, if different subgroups might respond differently to the policy treatment, the experiment must be designed to systemmatically show this, rather than allowing different subgroups to self-select into and out of certain aspects of the policy treatment.

The implementation model that parallels these ideas stresses that, when the relationship between those implementing a policy and those who are the "clients" (that is, target group) cannot be adequately standardized or controlled, implementation may be problemmatic. An example is Berman's (1978, p. 175) discussion of features of social-service programs that have been pointed to as sources of implementation difficulty:

> First, the delivery of the social service ... consists of the continuing interactions over time between a professional deliverer and a recipient of the service. These bilateral interactions ... require the "intensive" use of professional techniques whose "selection, combination, and order of application are determined by feedback from the [client]" (Thompson, 1967, p. 17). In this situation, analysts cannot assume projects can, will, or should be implemented uniformly across individual deliverers.

Just as the experimental design model is not amenable to the notion of "subjects" interacting with "experimenters" and influencing the character of the treatment to which they are exposed, so implementation theory exhibits concern over street-level bureaucrat/client encounters in the implementation process. The character of the policy being implemented can be changed in significant ways as a result of bureaucratic discretion at lower levels and pressures from powerful client or constituency groups.

These ideas are closely related to the third feature of the evaluation research paradigm—the concern for a controlled setting. I do not mean here the use of control groups in the sense of experimental design. Rather, I refer to the stipulation, crucial to the experimental paradigm, that those conducting the experiment and the context in which it is conducted be as neutral as possible so that any observed effects on the experimental subjects are clearly attributable to the treatment variable. The validity of the experimental paradigm is critically threatened if the experimenter is biased, interactive with the experimental subjects, or if the setting for administration of the experiment interferes in any way with the treatment itself.

These principles are mirrored in implementation theory. Successful implementation is viewed as being critically dependent on administrative agents who are in accord with the objectives of the policy, that is, who will not derail implementation because their own values and self-interests conflict with it. In the experimental paradigm, the notion of a neutral setting suggests not only that there are no interactive effects between experimenter and subject, but also that the experimenter is scientifically objective and detached. Translated into implementation theory, the neutrality principle takes on a slightly different cast. It requires that administrators be "sufficiently committed" so they will enforce regulations "in the face of resistance from target groups and from public officials reluctant to make the mandated changes .... Thus it is extremely important that implementation be assigned to agencies whose policy orientation is consistent with the statute and which will accord the new program high priority" (Sabatier and Mazmanian, 1979, p. 488).

In short, a conflictual, politicized setting is anathema to the classic model of implementation, just as turbulent, politicized settings posed problems for evaluation researchers (Weiss, 1970; Williams and Evans, 1972). A politicized, conflictual setting may mean that the policy cannot be implemented precisely as specified, or that the experimental evaluation cannot be conducted precisely as designed. The principle of a controlled, neutral setting is thus an important value in both the classic model of implementation theory and the classic paradigm of evaluation research. Other researchers have noted these tendencies as well, and have linked experimental design and classic implementation theory to the Weberian model of organization. Wolkon (1971), for example, discusses the "control" requirements of traditional evaluation research, and ties this to a Weberian conception of the agency being studied. And Nakamura and Small-wood (1980) argue that initial approaches to implementation were influenced by the classical model of administration—a model stressing a "rigid, machine-like hierarchical structure," clearly specified goals, specific directives to imple-mentors, and neutral, technically efficient administration.

It is important to note that Nakamura and Smallwood (1980) see this under-standing of implementation as going through a process of change. They argue that studies of decision making and organizational behavior showed the over-simplicity of the classical model, and that students of implementation have renewed their efforts to capture the complexities of implementation processes.

Implementation research is indeed changing. But this change does not involve the *supplanting* of the classical model. Rather, what we now have are two alternative models of implementation—models based on very different assumptions and values.

These competing models are perhaps best summarized by Berman (1980). The first, which Berman calls *programmed implementation*, corresponds to the understanding of implementation developed so far in this chapter—one that parallels evaluation research in its concern for goal clarity, compliance, and controlled settings.

> The programmed approach calls for "clarity, precision, comprehensive-ness . . . " Once the decision is taken preprogrammed implementation procedures are supposed to be followed by all levels of the organiza-tion or government involved.

> The programmed approach diagnoses implementation problems as arising from at least three sources: (1) ambiguity in policy goals result-ing in or caused by misunderstanding, confusion, or value conflict; (2) participation of too many actors with overlapping authority; and (3) implementers' resistance, ineffectualness, or inefficiency. (Berman, 1980, p. 208)

The following section examines the alternative to the classic, or programmed, implementation model, and traces developments that have yielded a different model of policy evaluation.

"Adaptive" Implementation and Qualitative/Process
Evaluation Approaches: Paradigmatic Partners

In marked contrast with the *programmed* implementation model outlined in the preceding section is the model Berman (1980) calls *adaptive* implementation.

> The ideal of adaptive implementation is the establishment of a process that allows policy to be modified, specified, and revised—in a word, adapted—according to the unfolding interaction of the policy with its institutional setting . . . it would look more like a disorderly learning process than a predictable procedure. (Berman, 1980, p. 211)

A number of developments contributed to the emergence of the adaptive model of implementation. Nakamura and Smallwood (1980) point to analysts such as Van Meter and Van Horn (1975), McLaughlin (1976), Bardach (1977) and Radin (1977), who characterized some of the personal and bureaucratic complexities that are an inevitable part of the implementation process, directed attention away from a machine-like model of implementation, and emphasized the participants' definition of the situation as a useful variable in designing implementation strategies. Studies of the important role of lower-level discretion in organizational change (Lipsky, 1976; Prottas, 1978) have also contributed to the adaptive model. Similarly, studies of the ways in which innovations are "reinvented" as they are applied (Rogers and Shoemaker, 1971; Rogers, 1978) have reinforced the importance of an adaptive view of implementation processes. Finally, the continuing influence of organization theorists who evaluate rigid, hierarchical models of organization (Ostrom, 1973) and emphasize a decentralized, flexible, and adaptive mode of organizational learning (Lindblom, 1965) has undoubtedly contributed to the model of adaptive implementation as well.

Notice that adaptive implementation eschews many of the principles of the experimental-design paradigm. A participatory orientation replaces the theme of predetermined, standardized treatment being administered to defined target groups. Goal specification becomes a problem rather than a value. Change, in both the policy (that is treatment/intervention) and the implementing organization (experimental setting), is a value rather than a problem. "Disorderly learning," in short, is the characteristic of adaptive implementation.

It should be seen as no accident that development of adaptive implementation has gone hand-in-hand with development of a paradigm change in evaluation research—a change that has generated considerable interest in qualitative methodology and process evaluation approaches (Patton, 1980; Palumbo and Sharp, 1980). Patton's (1980) review of the principles underlying qualitative evaluation methods illustrates nicely the contrasts with the experimental-design paradigm, and the parallels with adaptive implementation. First, the qualitative approach takes a holistic view:

> The holistic approach assumes that . . . a description and understanding
> of a program's context is essential for understanding the program . . . In
> contrast to experimental designs which manipulate and measure the
> relationships among a few carefully selected and narrowly defined
> variables, the holistic approach . . . is open to gathering data on any
> number of aspects of the setting under study in order to put together
> a complete picture of the social dynamic of a particular situation or
> program. (Patton, 1980, p. 40)

Rather than depending on a neutral, nonpolitical setting, qualitative evaluation
emphasizes the complex social and political dynamics of an implementation
situation, and the changes in understanding of the policy that may result.

Second, the qualitative approach is inductive. "The strategy in qualitative
designs is to allow the important dimensions to emerge from analysis of the
cases under study *without presupposing in advance what those important
dimensions will be*" (Patton, 1980, p. 40). Inductive research contrasts sharply
with the goal specification principle of the classic models of both evaluation
and implementation. It fits nicely with adaptive implementation, which assumes
that the meaning and purpose of the policy emerges out of the "unfolding interaction of the policy with its institutional setting (Berman, 1980, p. 211)."

Finally, qualitative evaluation is "naturalistic inquiry," which has to do
with a respect for naturally occurring, evolutionary processes and an avoidance
of manipulative, interventionist strategies. This principle contrasts with the
standardization and control that experimental design and programmed implementation require.

One of the most important forms of evaluation for which qualitative
strategies are particularly appropriate is process evaluation—an alternative
to the experimental design-based, impact-oriented model of evaluation. Process
evaluation involves a detailed description of how policies actually are implemented (or how programs actually work), toward the purpose of understanding
how outcomes are generated.

> The process evaluator sets out to understand and document the day-to-
> day reality of the setting or settings under study . . . Process evaluations
> look not only at formal activities and anticipated outcomes, but they
> also investigate informal patterns and unanticipated consequences . . .
> Finally, process evaluations usually include perceptions of people close
> to the program about how things are going. (Patton, 1980, pp. 60–61)

This brief review of adaptive implementation and process/qualitative
approaches to policy evaluation is intended to show how the two parallel each
other, and how they contrast with the classic models of evaluation and implementation. In sketching out the contrasts between programmed and adaptive
implementation, Berman does not attempt to show that one is inherently
superior to the other. Rather, the theme of his analysis is the need to *match*

implementation strategy to policy situation. Specifically, Berman (1980) argues that programmed implementation is only appropriate where the policy calls for incremental rather than major change, where the theory underlying the policy is certain, where there is little conflict over the policy's goals, where the institutional setting is "tightly coupled," and where the environment is stable. When any of these characteristics is not present, one needs to move toward a more adaptive strategy. In short, the idea is that implementation failure occurs if there is a mismatch between characteristics of the policy situation and the type of implementation strategy used.

Berman takes a pragmatic approach to the choice of implementation models. The idea is to choose that approach which works best, given the policy situation. In the case analysis that follows, a slightly different lesson is to be learned. The case is meant to illustrate how the different models of implementation and evaluation may have a substantive impact on the conclusions drawn from a particular implementation experience. Programmed and adaptive models are definitely normative and conceptual models from which evaluators of implementation must choose. The choice is likely to have a substantial impact on the kinds of questions that are asked and the kinds of conclusions reached concerning a particular implementation situation.

Choosing an Evaluation/Implementation Model to Guide Analysis: The Case of Citizen Participation in Midtown

One of the most significant developments in urban politics and administration during the last twenty years has been the proliferation of policies intended to enhance citizen participation in local government. Although the furor over citizen participation generated by the Community Action Program may have passed from the scene, the consumer movement, the increased attention being paid to urban neighborhoods, and requirements of federal funding programs have sustained interest in policy initiatives to increase citizen participation (Langton, 1978). Those citizen-participation policies which have been attempted range from ombudsmen and central complaint offices to town-hall meetings, neighborhood service centers, and appointed advisory boards or elected advisory councils (Cole, 1974).

Communities that commit themselves to major policy innovations in citizen participation have a need to know how such initiatives are being implemented. But to determine whether the policy has been successfully implemented, one needs to have some conception of what successful implementation entails. Furthermore, as the preceding section indicates, models of implementation are likely to be closely linked to models of evaluation.

This section is intended to show that a choice of evaluation and implementation analysis is likely to have a substantive impact on what is learned from a policy implementation experience. It is based on case material from an evaluation project currently being undertaken in a city in the mountain plains region. I use the pseudonym *Midtown* to protect the anonymity of those who are serving as informants in the study.

Midtown, a community of about 260,000 people, has a council-manager form of government. There are only five city commissioners (council members), one of whom serves as mayor, and all of whom are elected at large. The community has a substantial minority population, largely concentrated in the northeast section of the city.

In the mid-1970s, a series of events led to the adoption of an innovative policy to enhance citizen participation in Midtown. For some time, there had been concern about the lack of a formal structure for grass-roots input to the city commission, an understandable concern given the structure of local government in Midtown.

In the mid-1970s, a city commission was elected that included at least two members who had a strong orientation toward grass-roots citizen input. At the same time, the Community Development Block Grant (CDBG) program was being launched by the federal government, and cities were looking for help in interpreting requirements for citizen participation. One of the commissioners of Midtown (the one serving as mayor) attended a meeting at which federal officials were to explain the requirements of citizen participation to public officials in the region. As one informant described the situation, the mayor came back from the meeting irate, because the federal officials had seemed to downplay the importance of their own requirements, and to suggest that the cities set up any arrangement that would superficially meet the call for citizen participation in CDBG decision making. She returned, determined to do something more meaningful about creating a structure for citizen participation in local government deliberations.

The policy that emerged was one involving the creation of neighborhood councils. The entire city was divided into council areas, based on existing voting-precinct boundaries. Each neighborhood was to elect a nine-person council. Unlike special elections, which had notoriously low turnout, these elections were to be held as part of the regular city elections. Finally, each neighborhood council was to designate one member who would represent it on a central council (not to be confused with the regular city commission).

What were the councils to do, and how were they to do it? This is a crucial question, for it takes us into the critical area of goals, implementation strategies, and criteria for success. The official goals of the new citizen-participation policy can be found in Midtown's bylaws which stated that the purpose of the Neighborhood Council System (NCS) shall be to:

1. Provide for an equitable citizen participation system improving access to the governmental decision-making process for all citizens

2. Strengthen citizen input in a comprehensive planning program for social
    and physical development
3. Serve as an advisory agency to the city commission
4. Serve as a continuing source of information from citizens at a neighbor-
    hood level
5. Serve as a channel of communications from the city commission and the
    city administration to citizens

In addition to these goal statements, the description of a neighborhood council election process, procedures for filling vacancies, the designation of neighborhood council representatives to the central council, and other structural specifications, the bylaws indicate that the neighborhood council system will receive staff support from a secretariat, consisting of a coordinator appointed by the city manager with the concurrence of central council, and additional staff members hired by the coordinator with the approval of the city manager.

Finally, the bylaws provide an official listing of the functions, duties, and responsibilities of the neighborhood council system, which include zoning; code enforcement programs; physical improvements involving special assessments or relocation; location of area-service programs such as for the aged and health; exceptions to rules and ordinances, when legal provision is made, therefore, for such matters as tavern permits, signs, and so on, the annual operating budget of the city; the annual Capital Improvement program; federal grants for the poor and disadvantaged; budgets for block grant programs such as general revenue, sharing, and community development and other matters as may be designated from time to time by the board of city commissioners. The bylaws state that the councils need not act on all these items, but may initiate such recommendations as seem appropriate, and that each neighborhood council member is to represent the citizens in his neighborhood and to serve as a channel of information from the city to the citizens.

Midtown's neighborhood council system, now five years old, is still considered a very innovative one. Only a handful of cities across the country have citizen-participation policies this extensive, involving all neighborhoods, and using elections rather than appointment.

How should such a policy be evaluated? If one is to analyze the implementation of the policy, what questions should be asked? These questions confronted the author and a colleague as we engaged in discussions with city officials who were interested in evaluating the neighborhood council system. Out of our exploratory work and thinking, it became clear that the different models of evaluation and implementation (outlined in the preceding sections) would lead to different interpretations of the neighborhood council experience in Midtown.

The first difference between a classical/programmed approach and an adaptive/process approach has to do with the handling of policy goals. The classical, programmed approach, as we have seen, emphasizes the importance of clearly specified goals. If the policy statement (that is, legislation) does not embody clear goals, the evaluator's first task is to clarify them in consultation with policymakers. Hence, the policy implementation process would be viewed through the lens of officially defined goals (as initially stated or as developed for the evaluation). In contrast, the adaptive/process approach would look for the potentially conflicting, and ever-changing definition of policy purpose that different participants bring to it, and the impact of these differing perspectives on how implementation unfolds.

In Midtown, the neighborhood council policy, as officially promulgated, directs attention toward citizen input of an *advisory* nature. Although this goal is admittedly vague, discussions with city staff charged with assisting the councils showed that advisory input is taken to mean precisely what it denotes. Neighborhood councils are not meant to usurp any of the policymaking authority of the city commission. Their input is to be helpful, not authoritative; they are to provide information about neighborhood needs, but this does not carry with it the expectation that the city commission will necessarily act in accordance with neighborhood council recommendations.

Based on this goal definition, the policy and its implementation would be judged problemmatic, or outright unsuccessful, if neighborhood council members were to see their role as one of getting the commission to go their way on issues and if council members were to become alienated or vocally critical of commission decisions that did not reflect their recommendations. So far, it appears that council members generally understand and accept this goal. In our initial interviews, council members repeatedly emphasized that what is important is that they be heard—that "they [the city commissioners] may not always do what we want, but at least they listen."

Nevertheless, these interviews indicated that some council members have a slightly different understanding of the purpose of the neighborhood council system. For them, the NCS provides a structured means of stopping the city from doing things that are inappropriate, harmful to the neighborhood, or based on incompetent judgment. As an example, respondents told us about the Macon Street issue, which involved the city's plans to move the street (which now follows a bend in the river) back from the river, and to make the freed-up riverfront land available to private developers. The land along the river and Macon Street is now open space/parkland. A neighborhood council member got wind of this project from inquiries about an otherwise insignificant-looking item in the capital improvements budget. With the system of structured participants that the neighborhood council system provides, it was possible to mobilize a large number of citizens very quickly to defeat the proposal. Respondents' comments indicate that they believe the NCS should serve as a means of close monitoring of city activities and quick mobilization to block those deemed unwise—a goal that goes beyond the official understanding of the policy. An analytical framework that points us only to the officially promulgated goals of the policy would have blinded us to this goal, which some participants came to define as appropriate through their participation in the process—a goal against which they would tend to judge the NCS as a success.

Even if we move beyond the officially stated goals of the policy, the programmed and adaptive conceptions of implementation would tend to point us toward different phenomena. The programmed approach and its classic evaluation counterpart, as we have seen, views policy as an intervention that causes change in a specified target group. The policy itself (that is, the nature of the intervention) is not seen as changing in the process of administration. In contrast, the adaptive model, and its qualitative/process evaluation counterpart, emphasizes the adaption of the policy and the institutional setting. One expects, and looks for, change in *both* the policy and the entity that implements it. Furthermore, change in the institutional setting involves impacts not only on a narrowly specified target group, but also on a wide variety of implementing actors.

In Midtown, we found that an unstated, but very real policy goal from the perspective of city officials was the need to have a mechanism for removing some of the flak from city commissioners. Because there was no forum for discussion of neighborhood issues prior to the NCS (other than individual citizen appearances before city commission), commission meetings were often lengthy, trying experiences. For the city commission, then, an implicit goal of the NCS was to provide an alternate arena for citizens to voice problems and wrangle over issues so that commission meetings would not be so burdened with them. From this perspective, the policy's target group consists of the citizens of Midtown, especially those who are active, vocal participants on local issues. The policy is an intervention designed to change their behavior—specifically, to channel their participation to an alternative forum.

The adaptive implementation model would suggest, however, that we look for the developing understanding of the policy intervention that nonofficial actors hold, and consider change in the implementation setting as a whole, not just in a particular target group. From such a perspective, we are directed toward council members' belief that the policy intervention should have an impact *on the city commission*—that is, that the new policy should be viewed as a change in the entire structure of local governance, leading to city commissioners being more responsive to them. Furthermore, although the formal structure of the policy is set up to take some of the flak away from the city commission meeting forum and direct it toward an alternative one, neighborhood council members see the citizen-participation policy as a way of *increasing* citizen willingness to speak up before city council. City commission meetings are televised, and a respondent explained that when citizens see council members addressing the commission and being taken seriously, it demonstrates to them that they can do the same; and she indicates that she personally communicates this same theme to her neighbors.

That citizens and governmental officials have different views of the goals and target group for citizen-participation policies is not a new idea. Cole (1974), for example, argues that there is a citizen perspective and an official perspective on such policies—with the former having to do with better and more accountable services to the neighborhood; and the latter having to do with increased citizen trust and confidence in government, and lessened possibilities for disorder and violence. The crucial point here is that the choice of one or the other model of implementation and evaluation is likely to have an impact on which of these interpretations of the policy we see.

The programmed model, as we have seen, is also compliance oriented, viewing implementation as a preset machine that should function smoothly if implementors behave precisely as directed. Similarly, the classic model of evaluation assumes that there is tight control over the administration of the intervention, and proceeds to compare actual results with expected ones. In contrast, adaptive implementation and its counterpart process evaluation model focuses on the ways in which implementors "tinker" with the policy, the difficulties they have with it as initially formulated, and the ways in which they informally deal with these difficulties. Again, these different approaches would give us different interpretations of Midtown's citizen-participation experience, especially with respect to the issue of representation of neighborhood interests.

Taking the programmed view, we would ask whether participants are doing what they are supposed to do—whether the mechanisms and procedures stipulated in the bylaws are being followed. Are council members being elected from the appropriate neighborhoods? Have the specified number of seats been filled, and are the council members attending the meetings and enacting recommendations on the specified issue areas?

Such an approach would turn up some problems with Midtown's neighborhood council policy. Several of the neighborhoods have had difficulty keeping a full council—there are currently several vacancies. Furthermore, not all members have attended as stipulated. The neighborhood council system bylaws include a rule specifying that if a member misses three meetings in a year, that member is relieved of his seat and a replacement is appointed. This has occurred, and the set of council members now includes several appointed members.[2]

The adaptive implementation/process evaluation approach directs us toward a different type of representation problem, however. Here, the problem has less to do with whether seats are filled as specified, and more to do with confusion over the meaning of representation. From discussions with some neighborhood council members and support staff, it became clear that formal compliance with the procedures specified in the bylaws does not solve the question of representation. Instead, neighborhood council members are grappling with the question of what it means to "represent" their neighborhood.

A staff member, for example, indicated that citizens sometimes come to neighborhood council meetings to express their views, the council takes those and other considerations into account, and comes up with a recommendation that does not reflect those citizens' desires. Citizens then become disenchanted and ask, "How can they [the neighborhood council] represent me—they don't do what I say!"

In addition to this problem, neighborhood council members indicated their concern about acting as representatives for the neighborhood when, in fact, it is often difficult to know what neighborhood views are, since so few residents come to their meetings. To deal with this difficulty, at least one council has undertaken a number of outreach activities, including special notification to residents in the immediate vicinity of a proposed project, zoning change proposal, or problem. On the other hand, some neighborhood council members deal with the representation issue by adopting a trustee rather than an instructed delegate view of representation. They see themselves as exercising their own good judgment in identifying neighborhood problems and developing recommendations to help solve them.

The confusion over the meaning of representation extends to the functioning of the central council as well. After observing one meeting of the council, I spoke with a staff member about it. She indicated that there had been concern over the role of the central council representative with respect to neighborhood council action. Some neighborhood councils had stipulated that their central council representative was to act as an instructed delegate, and not to vote contrary to the vote taken on a given recommendation by the neighborhood council. Nevertheless, she indicated, at the meeting we observed, a couple of representatives had voted differently from the action taken by their council, and these switches had confused the proceedings and taken the meeting in a direction no one expected. In short, the group dynamic had yielded an outcome that would not have been predicted, given the formal structure that had been created.

As a final note, the choice of a classic evaluation based on a strong experimental design was one not open to us as we entered the Midtown situation. The policy had been launched full scale, with no built-in structure for experimentally designed evaluation. The program was implemented citywide from the start (not in a few neighborhoods matched against control-group neighborhoods), and no "before" data had been collected on variables that might later be examined as outcome measures in an "after" data collection. In a sense, then, the city officials in Midtown, whether consciously or not, did not approach this policy innovation as a social experiment in the classic sense. Rather, it appears that they viewed this policy as a more or less permanent change in the functioning of citizen participation in Midtown, and presumably assumed that any difficulties or advantages of the policy would emerge out of their experience with it.

Nevertheless, a quasi-experimental evaluation approach, coupled with an implementation analysis based on the programmed model, is still a possibility, and one that may appeal to city officials. Using survey research methods, for example, one could compare the responses of citizens aware of and involved in the neighborhood council system with those not, controlling for social status, political efficacy, and other factors likely to influence both their involvement and their responses on outcome measures. Given the formal and implicit goals of policymakers, outcome measures might include such variables as confidence in government, satisfaction with city services or other city policies, and belief in the accessibility of city government. In addition, system-level variables, such as the proportion of commission meeting time devoted to citizen input and the number of citizen complaints filed, could be examined on a before-and-after basis.

These are important questions, and to the extent that resources permit, we will undoubtedly pursue some of them in our evaluation. But they are *different* research questions from those which would be pursued with a process evaluation/adaptive implementation framework guiding us. In such a case, one would ask questions such as: What are the motivations of citizens who become involved as neighborhood council members? What are their initial expectations, and how do these change over time as they participate in the system? How have local officials responded to the neighborhood councils? Has there been any change over time in their understanding of what the neighborhood council system can and should accomplish? What kinds of issues have the councils addressed, and how have they gone about considering them and developing recommendations? What do participants see as the most important accomplishments and most important limitations of Midtown's innovative citizen-participation policy? These and many other "process" questions are important as well, and, as our initial in-depth interview strategy suggests, we are pursuing them also.

In sum, our response so far to the dilemma of choice between competing models of implementation and of policy evaluation has been one of eclecticism. By drawing from both pairs of models, we hope to learn as much about Midtown's policy implementation experience as each approach has to offer. But resource constraints, personal considerations, and other factors may mean that the eclectic approach is not always possible. It is important, therefore, to recognize that choice of one implementation/evaluation approach rather than the other may well have substantive implications. These brief case examples have, we hope, helped to illustrate some of these implications of that choice.

Notes

1. Some readers may object to references to implementation *theory*, because, as Berman (1978, p. 159) suggests, all the conceptual developments involving implementation "do not yet constitute a fully articulated framework,

let alone a theory." My purpose is not to argue that there are two fully developed, competing theories of implementation, but rather to show that there are two competing schools of thought on implementation, variously referred to as models or approaches. These competing models may be viewed as developing theories, but it is important to note, as Elmore (1978) does, that the use of the term *theory* with regard to implementation studies must, in any case, be used with care. The models of implementation developed so far are normative, descriptive, and heuristic—they are not theories in the strict scientific sense.

2. As a result of these problems, the city of Midtown had, even before the initiation of the current evaluation, undertaken a study of the problem of turnover in neighborhood councils.

References

Bardach, E. *The Implementation Game*. Cambridge, Mass.: MIT Press, 1977.

Berman, P. "The Study of Macro- and Micro-Implementation." *Public Policy* (Spring 1978):157-184.

_____. "Thinking about Programmed and Adaptive Implementation: Matching Strategies to Situations." In *Why Policies Succeed or Fail*, edited by H. Ingram and D. Mann, pp. 205-230. Beverly Hills, Calif.: Sage Publications.

Borus, M. *Measuring the Impact of Employment-Related Social Programs*. W.E. Upjohn Institute for Employment Research, 1979.

Cole, R. *Citizen Participation and the Urban Policy Process*. Lexington, Mass.: Lexington Books, D.C. Heath and Company, 1974.

Derthick, M. *New Towns In-Town*. Washington, D.C.: Urban Institute, 1972.

Elmore, R. "Organizational Models of Social Program Implementation." *Public Policy* (Spring 1978): 185-228.

Houston, T. "The Behavioral Sciences Impact-Effectiveness Model." In *Evaluating Social Programs*, edited by P. Rossi and W. Williams. New York: Seminar Press, 1972.

Langton, S. *Citizen Participation in America*. Lexington, Mass.: Lexington Books, D.C. Heath and Company, 1978.

Lindblom, C. *The Intelligence of Democracy*. New York: Free Press, 1965.

Lipsky, M. "Toward a Theory of Street-Level Bureaucracy." In *Theoretical Perspectives on Urban Politics*, edited by W. Hawley and M. Lipsky. Englewood Cliffs, N.J.: Prentice-Hall, 1976.

McLaughlin, M. "Implementation as Mutual Adaptation." In *Social Program Implementation*, edited by W. Williams and R. Elmore, Academic Press, 1976.

Moynihan, D. *Maximum Feasible Misunderstanding*. New York: Free Press, 1970.

Nakamura, R., and Smallwood, F. *The Politics of Policy Implementation*. New York: St. Martin's Press, 1980.

Ostrom, V. *The Intellectual Crisis in American Public Administration*. University, Ala.: The University of Alabama Press, 1973.

Palumbo, D., and Sharp, E. "Process Versus Impact Evaluation of Community Corrections." In *The Practice of Policy Evaluation*, edited by D. Nachmias. New York: St. Martin's Press, 1980.

Patton, M.Q. *Qualitative Evaluation Methods*. Beverly Hills, Calif.: Sage Publications, 1980.

Pressman, J., and A. Wildavsky. *Implementation*. Berkeley, Calif.: University of California Press, 1973.

Prottas, J. "The Power of the Street-Level Bureaucrat in Public Service Bureaucracies." *Urban Affairs Quarterly* (March 1978): 285-312.

Radin, B. *Implementation, Change, and the Federal Bureaucracy*. New York: Columbia University, Teachers College Press, 1977.

Rogers, E., and Shoemaker, F. *Communication of Innovations: A Cross Cultural Approach*. New York: Free Press, 1971.

Rogers, E. "Re-Invention during the Innovation Process." In *The Diffusion of Innovations: An Assessment*, edited by M. Radner et al. Evanston, Ill.: Northwestern University, 1978.

Sabatier, P., and Mazmanian, D. "The Conditions of Effective Implementation: A Guide to Accomplishing Policy Objectives." *Policy Analysis* (Fall, 1979): 481-505.

Van Meter, D., and Van Horn, C. "The Policy Implementation Process: A Conceptual Framework," *Administration and Society*, February, 1975.

Weiss, C. "The Politicization of Evaluation Research," *Journal of Social Issues* (Autumn 1970):57-68.

―――――. *Evaluation Research*. Englewood Cliffs, N.J.: Prentice-Hall, 1972.

Williams, W., and Evans, J. "The Politics of Evaluation: The Case of Head Start." In *Evaluating Social Programs*, edited by P. Rossi and W. Williams. New York: Seminar Press, 1972.

Wolkon, G. "Consent, Cooperation, and Control in Rehabilitation Research." In *The Organization, Management and Tactics of Social Research*, edited by R. O'Toole. Cambridge, Mass.: Schenkman.

**Part IV
Using Evaluation to
Improve Implementation**

10 Dealing with Changes in a Program's Goals and Design: Methods from a Formative Evaluation of the Florida Linkage System

Garrett R. Foster and
Peter A. Easton

What role can formative evaluation play in reformulating initial program goals and design during the development and implementation of a new program? Evidence from the literature on educational innovation and from the current experience of the Florida Linkage System (FLS), a project designed to develop problem-solving capabilities in local schools, indicates that reconsideration of objectives and methods in the course of implementation is a critical need of most change projects. But existing models of formative evaluation provide little guidance for such an undertaking. In this chapter, the need for formative evaluation of program goals and design is argued, and the methods developed to meet this need in the context of a recently completed project are presented.

The Problem

Recent literature on educational program implementation has placed emphasis on the changes that the goals and methods of innovative programs typically undergo—or need to undergo—in the course of implementation, and on the processes of mutual adaptation necessary for staff and participants to adjust the initial program design to their maturing perceptions of local needs and potentials (Berman and McLaughlin, 1975; Kritek, 1976; Fullan and Pomfret, 1977).

Evidence from the Rand study of federally funded programs of educational innovation (Berman and McLaughlin, 1975) and from our own work with the dissemination and diffusion of educational research and development (Foster et al., 1979) indicates not only that goal priorities and appreciations of program methodology often change in the course of implementation, but also that the perceptions of different subgroups of project-related personnel may shift in markedly different directions.

We have argued elsewhere that this situation has important implications for the practice of evaluation (Foster and Easton, 1980b). It is evident that a summative evaluation which assesses program worth in terms of an outmoded set of goals, or attempts to explain results on the basis of an outmoded version of the program design, risks passing very wide of the mark. Detailed descriptions of the changes that have taken place in the objectives and methods of

119

the program are needed to serve as a basis for these overall judgments. Such data could be provided by systematic formative evaluation of program goals and design carried out during the course of implementation—and the effort to chronicle these changes would seem potentially as useful to supervisory staff and program participants as to summative evaluators. Yet present evaluation methodology does not provide us with a clear approach for adjusting to changes in the goals and methods of a program or for helping those concerned with the program articulate and direct this process.

One method for the formative evaluation of program goals and design has been worked out in the framework of an evaluation of the Florida Linkage System (FLS). The FLS is a statewide program designed to assist local school personnel in the identification of instructional and organizational problems within their schools and in the selection and adaptation of appropriate solutions. In this chapter, we describe the methods developed for adjusting the goals and design of the FLS and discuss the results and implications of their application. The following section is devoted to a brief description of the Florida Linkage System itself. Ensuing sections deal with the development and application of a formative methodology for adjusting program goals and design during the implementation stage.

The Florida Linkage System

The Florida Linkage System was established in 1976 in order to provide Florida schools with access to educational research and development products adapted to local needs and to assist them in developing the capacity to analyze and resolve their own instructional or organizational problems. The system links local schools to state and university agencies able to provide training and research products on request and is coordinated by the Office of Dissemination and Diffusion of the state Department of Education.

Each participating school selects from among its faculty and staff a cadre of internal change agents, known as a *facilitating team*, who receive training in group problem resolution processes and select and implement appropriate solutions. *Linkage agents*, located in regional teacher-education centers, maintain contact with several project schools in order to support local facilitators, channel their requests to the Office of Dissemination and Diffusion, and help them utilize to best advantage the training and research and development resources that the system makes available.

The FLS model is based on a *linkage theory* of educational dissemination and diffusion principally elaborated by Robert Havelock of the University of Michigan (Havelock, 1971). Linkage theory combines elements of the social interaction, research and development, and problem-solving models of educational diffusion that have been advanced in the last thirty years. It stresses the importance of connecting schools with external sources of support in the research and development community and at the same time promoting local faculty participation in identifying the instructional or organizational problems within the schools that research products can help resolve. The combining of these various approaches is counted on to result in better utilization of educational research and development.

The FLS model prescribes a series of steps by which local schools can elect to participate in the system, form their own facilitating teams, identify their principal instructional (or organizational) problems, and obtain outside support in addressing them. Between 1976 and 1979, the system was field tested in twenty-eight primary schools located in sixteen counties across the state of Florida. Responsibility for directing formative and summative evaluation of the Florida Linkage System was given to staff of the Florida State University College of Education. The methods described in this chapter were developed in the course of that evaluation, which spanned the entire life of the project.

Methods and Instruments

A set of instruments was designed by the evaluation team for administration to staff and participants at various levels of the FLS in order to enlist their assistance in reexamining the goals and model of the program in light of their intervening experience. The instruments included a goal analysis questionnaire, a model update questionnaire, and a facilitator survey. The process involved in developing and administering these instruments necessitated a large measure of participation and reflection by project staff and was itself part and parcel of our methodology of formative evaluation. We will consequently present it in some detail before describing each of the three questionnaires.

Instrument Development and Administration

The formative evaluation process consisted of five steps, each involving consultation with project staff. The initial step concerned definition of the goals and the model of the FLS. As is so often the case with educational and social-change projects, there existed no single exposition of FLS objectives and methods that was universally accepted or used. Instead, there were a number of overlapping and more or less congruent versions presented in different project documents. The first task for the evaluators was, therefore, to identify the documents thought to contain the essentials of FLS methodology and to review this choice with project staff.

Once a coherent version of the initial goals and model of the project had been settled on, the instruments themselves could be defined. Each was designed to elicit the judgment of project personnel concerning the relative importance and practicality of different goals, model components, and project tasks. The entire set of instruments was reviewed with FLS staff and field tested on a small sample before administration.

The fourth step involved administering the questionnaires to the appropriate groups of respondents. Wherever feasible, the evaluation team opted for direct contact with the respondents in a group setting in order to allow for feedback about questionnaire content and to emphasize the formative character of the activity. The goal and model analysis instruments were administered in separate group settings to FLS staff, linkers, and members of the FLS advisory boards. Only local school personnel received mail-in goal analysis questionnaires, and the nature and purpose of these questionnaires were discussed with them by the linkers, most of whom had previously participated in a round-table group evaluation on the same theme.

The last step involved analysis and communication of the results of the questionnaires. In general, data were simplified in two ways to ensure ease of interpretation:

Responses to scales of attitude or opinion (for example, about the importance or practicality of different goals) were dichotomized.

Data were then summarized in terms of group consensus, operationally defined as agreement by two-thirds of a given group of respondents; that is, the goal statements and model components judged "important" or "practicable" by two-thirds of the respondents were distinguished from those judged "unimportant" or "impracticable" by a two-thirds majority and from those goals eliciting no such censensus in either direction.

It was consequently possible to calculate in a relatively short time the results of each of the questionnaires and to feed this information back to the respondents for discussion and program revision. The comments and program revisions were also summarized in a written report of results (Foster et al., 1979).

Goal Analysis Questionnaire

The first of the instruments was a "goal analysis questionnaire," administered to those of the project staff and related policymaking bodies who were most acquainted with FLS goals and objectives: the central project staff, members of two FLS advisory boards, the teacher-education center linkers, and principals of the participating schools. The goal analysis questionnaire listed twenty-nine specific goals subsumed under seven broad goal categories, all culled from FLS project documents. Some of the goal statements overlapped but the redundancies were allowed to stand in order to determine which phrasing or formulation was preferred.

The goal analysis questionnaire was divided into two parts. In the first, respondents were asked to rate on separate six-point Likert-type scales, the extent to which each goal should be used as a criterion for an upcoming summative evaluation and the extent to which each should be emphasized in future administration of the project. The "future emphasis" scale was added in order to elicit respondents' feelings about the importance of program goals independently of the immediate context of accountability. Space was also provided for listing other goals that individuals judged relevant or critical.

The second part of the goal analysis questionnaire was designed to elicit respondents' judgment of the relative importance of the broad goal categories. Fifteen paired comparisons were used to establish a ranking among the principal goal groups.

The first part of the goal analysis questionnaire was scored by the two-thirds consensus method in order to facilitate presentation of the results of FLS staff and participants and to clarify common-sense interpretation of the findings. Results of the paired comparison of the major goal clusters were analyzed to yield a quasi-equal-interval ranking of these general objectives by the overall group of respondents and by each of the subgroups.

Model Update Questionnaire

The second instrument developed for formative evaluation of program input was a model update questionnaire, derived from an analysis of project documents, which detailed the specific steps prescribed by the FLS for the identification of school-level programs, the selection of appropriate solutions, and the implementation of new programs. The entire exercise of developing, administrating, and interpreting the model update questionnaire was conceived of as a formative process that would both enable field staff to articulate their evaluations of program design and help project management and advisors better understand how the FLS model was in fact being operationalized at the local school level. It was hoped that the activity would result in a better fit between the model and the realities of implementation in the field.

After analysis of the available documentation and progressive refinement of the results with project staff, model elements were identified and sorted into four areas of FLS activity: systematic problem solving, internal facilitation, external linkage, and external assistance. These then served as a basis for design of a model update instrument.

In the section of the instrument dealing with systematic problem solving, respondents were asked to indicate which of the steps in the prescribed process should be retained, which modified, and which deleted. In addition, each stage in the FLS problem-solving method was rated to determine its *importance* to the success of local problem solving and its *practicality* in terms of difficulty, effort, and cost of implementation.

The sections on internal facilitation and external linkage presented a list of very specific activities (for example, "periodically stimulate interest in emerging educational innovations") prescribed by the model for accomplishment within the school or at the district level. Respondents were asked to indicate who, (facilitator, linker, other), if anyone, should take primary responsibility for each of the activities.

Finally, in the section on external resources and assistance, judgments were requested as to the appropriate level of involvement of different agents (parents, district personnel, consultants, and so on) at each of the major stages of the local problem-solving process.

Only groups immediately involved in implementation of the FLS model were considered appropriate respondents for the questionnaire. These included project staff, district linkers, and school facilitating teams. A separate survey was developed for the latter group. As a consequence, the model update questionnaire was administered only to project staff and district linkers.

Survey of Local School Personnel

The third and last instrument in the series, a facilitator survey, was designed along the lines of the model update questionnaire for administration to members of each school's facilitating team. Seven tasks that constitute the operational version of the problem-solving model were delineated on the basis of an analysis of FLS documents, and the facilitators were asked to indicate, via a series of scales, whether the task had in fact been implemented, how practical and useful they perceived it to be, and how important the help of the linker and other support personnel had been in its accomplishment.

Facilitating teams from twenty-four schools were surveyed. Actual team composition varied from school to school, but all teams were composed of at least one administrator and two teachers. The surveys were distributed and explained to facilitators by the linkers, and mailed in after completion by the respondents. Seventy-four responses were obtained from the twenty-four schools.

Results

We turn now to a brief examination of the results obtained by the application of our methods: the kind of data actually produced by each instrument, the use and utility of this information, and the principal pitfalls encountered in design, administration, and interpretation.

Data from the Individual Instruments

As a result of the model update activity, the conceptual specification of the FLS model was modified in several important respects. Based on their experience, respondents suggested ways of simplifying the model format. Two steps in the problem-identification process were dropped and another was incorporated into activities already specified by the model. Several aspects of the model were consolidated to better reflect the practice found most useful in the field.

Results from the goal analysis questionnaire were used to identify the objectives that policymakers, project staff, and contract personnel judged to be most central to the mission of the FLS. They thus provided one basis for organizing the summative evaluation of the project. Thirteen of the twenty-nine goals abstracted from FLS documentation were deemed appropriate as summative evaluation criteria by at least two-thirds of the respondents. Significantly, among those dropped were a number of objectives relating to student performance; there was consensus among all groups that this dimension of evaluation should be postponed until implementation had been completed at the school level.

In addition, the goal analysis questionnaire provided very instructive data on differences in perceptions among the various subgroups of respondents, and these data were a source of useful feedback between policymaking and field personnel. For example, results of the questionnaire made it evident the teacher-education center linkers placed greatest emphasis on the development of problem-solving and communication skills at the local level. The advisory group, on the other hand, tended to emphasize the importance of research and development dissemination, while project staff gave more weight to the creation of institutional linkages between local schools and resource centers. Discussion of these results with the respondents helped develop greater unity of purpose in the project and increased the interest of all participating groups in the accomplishment of goals and in the process of summative evaluation.

Data from the facilitator survey furnished a local school perspective on FLS methods and so provided a complement to the results of the model update and goal analysis questionnaires and a basis of comparison with these findings. Facilitators' judgments of the utility of different steps in the FLS process proved essentially congruent with the perceptions of the other groups reflected in the goal analysis questionnaire (though most congruent with those of the linkers). Their responses also pinpointed a component of the model (the "search for alternative solutions") that needed simplification and redesigning.

Utility of the Instruments

Overall, the three surveys—the goal analysis, the model update, and the facilitator survey—furnished useful and complementary information and provided a means and an occasion for critical review of the basic elements of the Florida Linkage System by those most closely involved.

We discovered, however, that we had not extended the use of our methods far enough up the policymaking ladder. Whereas district- and project-level personnel concerned with FLS policy took an active part in the formative evaluation activities, division heads within the state Department of Education were not explicitly involved. We had counted on project management keeping their superiors apprised of the changing complexion of FLS goals and methods; but this communication link turned out to be weaker than anticipated, partly because state-level officials were responsible for so many projects of similar scope that they were unlikely to give much attention to the interim evolution of the FLS without more organized prompting. As a consequence, top-level policymakers ended up reaching decisions about the continuation of the project on the basis of a by then outmoded version of its design, and state support was withdrawn at precisely the moment when project, district, and local personnel had developed a large degree of "ownership" of the undertaking and interest in its success. The lesson for future evaluation efforts seems to be that some form of participation by top-level policymakers in model update and goal analysis activities should be explicitly organized from the outset.

Despite this major shortcoming in the organization of the evaluation—which, in a sense, simply confirms the importance of update and goal analysis—use of the methods proved beneficial for the project in several respects. First, as mentioned earlier, the results brought about a reversal of the attitude that the project should be evaluated strictly in terms of student performance. The data also brought to light a shift from an emphasis on product utilization to one on school process and at the same time identified those process goals which were considered important criteria for evaluation. These were, in fact, used as the basis for summative evaluation. Finally, and as a side effect, the evaluation process provided a vehicle for intercommunication among field staff about the techniques found most effective in the course of implementation. While furnishing feedback to project management about the adequacy of goals and model components, district-level linkers also shared and refined their individual evaluations of implementation methods.

Conclusions

The goal analysis and model update activities described in this chapter proved to be a useful means for adjusting the official objectives and methods of the Florida Linkage System to the changing reality of the project and the changing perceptions of those involved. As such, they provide a rough first approximation of a methodology for formative evaluation of project goals and design.

The essential steps in this process can be summarized as follows. It should be emphasized that the process must be iterative and that source documents, proposed instruments, and preliminary findings need to be checked with project staff at every step along the way.

1. Assemble existing documention on project goals and model.
2. Identify personnel groups actively involved in or concerned with the enunciation of project goals and the implementation of the project model: policymakers, project staff, and field staff constitute three critical categories.

3. Perform a content analysis of documentation in order to identify the various goals and the set and sequence of model components.
4. Design instruments to elicit the judgment of respondent groups as to the current (or future) importance, utility, and practicality of the objectives and model components identified.
5. Administer the instruments and, insofar as possible, conduct a preliminary analysis with the participants so that group reactions to the emerging judgments may also be recorded.
6. Perform a further analysis of results, scoring scaled results in a manner that enhances realiability and ease of common-sense interpretation.
7. Feed back all results to respondents in a group session, if possible, for interpretation and revision of goal priorities and model characteristics.
8. Make a written report of results and interpretation and offer it as input to the summative evaluation and to planning and policy-setting personnel.

Our experience suggests that a distinction should be maintained between analysis of project goals and reconsideration of the project model, and that separate instruments should probably be used for the two purposes. Furthermore, the same instrument or set of instruments may not be appropriate for all respondent groups. In the FLS case, the cadre of local change agents (school-level facilitating team) had a much more concrete and detailed responsibility for local project activities and much less exposure to its conceptualization than project staff and policymakers. This difference in experience and perspective suggested separate instrumentation, but provided, as mentioned earlier, a control for certain sources of bias in the results.

Our experience likewise suggests that the participation of each group of project-related personnel in evaluation and feedback activities must be as carefully planned in advance as the instruments themselves. In particular, top-level policymakers need to be included in one part or another of the goal analysis and model update exercises.

The overall "payoff" for formative evaluation or program goals and design during the course of implementation seems to use to more than compensate for the extra effort involved. Several types of benefits proved especially important in the context of the Florida Linkage System. Goal analysis and model update activities brought to light and articulated a shift in emphasis from student performance and product utilization objectives to an increased concern with school process. Data on this evolution in the conception of the program had important implications both for summative evaluation and for educational theory. At the same time, the mechanisms for feedback and critical review of program design afforded project staff an opportunity to "compare notes" and refine their methods of intervention.

Further refinements of the approach are certainly needed. The particulars of our instrumentation relate to a specific sphere of activity—state-supported educational innovation—but goal analysis and model update appear to be a generic need to change projects, and an appropriate methodology can best be shaped with input from a variety of settings.

References

Berman, P., and McLaughlin, M.W. *Federal Programs Supporting Educational Change.* Santa Monica, Calif.: Rand Corporation, 1975.

Foster, G.R., and Easton, P. "Field-Testing the Linkage Model of Educational Innovation." Paper presented to the annual conference of the American Educational Research Association, Boston, Mass., April, 1980a.

_____. "Updating the Model and Goals of an Educational Change Program: A Third Dimension of Formative Evaluation." *CEDR Quarterly,* June, 1980b.

Foster, GR.; Richardson, G.; Papagiannis, M.; and Easton, P. *Evaluation Studies for the Florida Linkage System.* Tallahassee, Florida: Florida Department of Education, 1979.

Fullan, M.E., and Pomfret, A. "Research on Curriculum and Instruction Implementation." *Review of Educational Research* 47, no. 1 (1977):335-397.

Havelock, R.G. *Planning for Innovations through Dissemination and Utilization of Knowledge.* Ann Arbor, Michigan: Institute for Social Research, Michigan State University, 1971.

Kritek, W.J. "Lessons from the Literature on Implementation." *Educational Administration Quarterly* 12, no. 3 (1976):86-102.

11

Optimizing Child-Welfare Policy through Research and Demonstration Projects

Lenore Olsen

Current child-welfare policy focuses on the need to plan permanency for foster-care children, particularly for those "hard-to-place" children who have grown up lost in the foster-care system. This policy has been implemented through several research and demonstration projects funded by the federal government in the last few years. A key thesis of this chapter is that these research and demonstration projects provide us with an opportunity to experiment with the implementation of policy, so that policy may be optimized. This chapter will discuss one such project, a coordinated four-county project in northeastern Ohio, a case study that illustrates three policy implementation issues: (1) the role of administrators and staff in goal setting, (2) original versus emergent goals, and (3) the role of evaluation.

In order to set a framework for this discussion, I will first review the current policy of planning permanency for children in foster care. Following this review, I will persent a brief history of the project in order to set the context for discussing how the policy of permanency was implemented for children in the foster-care system.

Review of Current Policy

A major theme in child-welfare policy today is the emphasis on permanency for all children in foster case. This theme has been widely discussed in the literature and has been the target of recent research and demonstration projects (National Center on Child Abuse and Neglect, 1979). In the majority of these discussions, the assumption has been made that a plan for permanency entails either returning the child to his home or, if this is not possible, placing the child for adoption. Increased efforts to place so-called hard-to-place children (older children, minority-group children, and children with handicaps) for

Partial support for this chapter was received from the Human Services Design Laboratory, School of Applied Social Sciences, Case Western Reserve University, which received funding from the Office of Child Development, United States Department of Health, Education, and Welfare, to conduct the evaluation study on which this chapter is based. The contributions of Lawrence Pitterman, Dorothy Faller, Paula Smith, and Shira Most to the original evaluation project are gratefully acknowledged.

129

adoption are a result of the heightened concern about permanency for all children. For those children who cannot be returned to their own homes, adoption is regarded as the best alternative, for it gives the child a home in which permanent attachments can be formed without the threat of removal (Fanshel and Shinn, 1978; Knitzer and Allen, 1978). The approach of finding adoptive homes for these children is further advocated because of a belief that long-term foster care may be detrimental to the child:

> We are not completely sure that continued tenure in foster care over extended periods is not in itself harmful to children . . . We would therefore support efforts to free children for adoption if strong efforts to restore natural parents to effective functioning are not successful. (Fanshel and Shinn, 1978, pp. 479–480)

The policy of permanency for all foster-care children has been implemented through the use of several strategies that minimize foster-care "drift." These strategies have been designed to protect against children becoming lost in the system and to develop alternatives that will ensure permanency for a greater number of children. Such strategies include periodic case reviews and case monitoring, use of service contracts, adoption subsidies, and special projects to develop permanent living situations for foster-care children. The following section discusses one such demonstration project that was designed to develop permanent homes for handicapped children.

The District Eleven Adoption Project

The District Eleven Adoption Project was funded by the Office of Child Development, Department of Health, Education, and Welfare, for a three-year period to demonstrate whether special efforts directed toward handicapped children in foster care would increase their chances for adoptive placement. As Martin Rein notes, "a major purpose of demonstration projects is to test the validity of ideas which claim to improve the services and policies of established institutions" (Rein, 1970).

Four county-level child-welfare agencies joined together in a coordinated effort to implement this project. Each of the four participating agencies allocated one staff person to the project to be responsible for referral of children in their individual counties to the project and for provision of services to those children as well as to potential adoptive families. The project coordinator and secretary were located in the offices of the lead agency, with the adoption workers stationed in each of their respective county agencies. Administrators from the four agencies joined together to form a policy-setting advisory board that provided the project with overall direction and administrative support for implementation of the project in the individual agencies.

Collection of baseline information for five years preceding the project allowed for a before-and-after design in which the implementation of policy could be evaluated. In addition, a process-focused evaluation, designed to assess the coordination among the agencies as it affected the implementation of the project, produced information about how the system was functioning. Both types of information were fed back to administrators and project staff on a periodic basis so that problems hindering implementation could be addressed and factors facilitating implementation could be strengthened during the course of the project.

A primary purpose of the project was to improve services not only for children referred to the project but also for all handicapped children in the four-county region. At the end of the three-year period, the percentage of handicapped children placed for adoption had increased from 29 percent to 44 percent. During this period, the agencies also began to place handicapped children for adoption who had been in agency care for a number of years. One of the most pronounced successes of the project was that it increased the percentage of families accepting handicapped children for adoption from 32 percent in 1975 to 58 percent in 1977. In addition, the project demonstrated an impact on the host agencies, particularly in raising awareness about the need to periodically review cases and in increasing knowledge about the resources available for adoptive placement of all foster-case children.

Implementing the Policy of Permanency

Goal Setting. As Deutscher (1977) notes in his discussion of the goal trap, goal setting may be a particular problem for innovative programs where one cannot be sure of what outcomes to expect. However, to find sources that are achievement oriented and to ask for evaluations of demonstration projects, one needs measurable goals by which to judge the success of a project. The process by which goals are set under these circumstances is especially critical for implementation, for it will determine how relevant and useful an evaluation of implementation will be. Setting relevant and meaningful goals can serve to focus project efforts on the most salient policy issues. For this ideal to be approached, however, requires early and extensive involvement of administrators and project staff in the identification of goals. This process of negotiating program goals, in which the evaluator, project staff, and administrators attempt to reach mutual agreement, should result in "goals which all parties find acceptable" (Deutscher, 1977). If this process is carried out, it can serve to optimize the conditions under which policy is implemented.

In the adoption project, an extensive series of meetings were held at the start of the project, between agency administrators, project staff, and evaluators. Although goals had been set in the proposal, this process allowed for review and limited modifications of the program goals. Modification occurred when the project coordinator, an experienced practitioner in the field, advocated a change in a goal that would result in a more realistic yardstick by which to measure the program's accomplishments. Moreover, this scrutiny helped illuminate the underlying purposes of the project and to identify some of its latent goals. These latent goals included such targets as changes in workers' attitudes about the "adoptability" of special-needs children and changes in administrative practices that hindered the process of planning permanency for children. These goals reflected a desire on the part of project staff to change the host system so that the policy of permanency could be more broadly implemented for a wider group of children beyond the specified target group (Rein, 1970; Weiss, 1973).

The discussions that emerged during this process of review and negotiation of original program goals set the tone for a working relationship between administrators, project staff, and evaluators in which the project's contribution to the policy of permanency could be meaningfully examined (Weiss, 1971). This relationship established a foundation from which the project could influence the policy of permanency for children in this foster-care system.

Changes in Goals. In applying goals to specific situations, redefinition and interpretation of the original goals usually is required. This process of reappraisal often leads to changes in the goals of the organization that more accurately represent the relationship between the organization and its environment. These changes may represent opportunities for programs to optimize policy, and for this reason should be encouraged.

The adoption project was originally designed to serve handicapped children, but as evaluative information about children in foster care was fed back to the project staff, it became clear that a much broader group of children was in need of service. These were children who had been in the system for a number of years, and for whom no permanent plans had been developed. Children from minority background were overrepresented in this backlog of cases. Project staff took it as their responsibility to relay this information to the agency workers assigned to the cases. Ultimately, these data provided the basis from which a spin-off project was implemented to serve the permanency needs of minority children. Thus, although the project had been originally designed to serve only handicapped children, in being responsive to its environment, the project's goals were expanded so that the project, in effect, became a watchdog for all children experiencing drift and impermanency. If the project staff had limited themselves to the original goal of serving only handicapped children, the policy of permanency would have been implemented in a more limited way.

Although the project expanded its purpose during the three-year demonstration period, its official goals were never changed. Perrow's (1961) delineation of official and operative goals is particularly useful for understanding this process of goal changing. Official goals, Perrow notes, address the general purpose of the organization, whereas operative goals "designate the ends sought through the actual operating policies of the organization" (Perrow, 1961). Although the general purpose of the adoption project was to plan permanence for handicapped children, the project actually sought to correct foster-care drift for all children. Thus, its operating procedures called for case reviews of all children who might be in need of permanency planning. Staff training was initiated to increase staff's awareness about the need to plan permanence and to expand their knowledge about how barriers to permanence might be overcome.

Perrow also says that operative goals are shaped by the dominant group and are reflective of critical task areas, the background characteristics of the dominant group, and the unofficial uses to which this group puts the organization. In this situation, the dominant group was the project staff, for they had daily responsibility for program implementation and, thus, had the greatest influence on project directions. The task area they came to see as most critical was that of coordinating the program with the agencies' clients. In defining this task area, they found that their professional backgrounds and experiences led them to broaden the purposes of the project so that the policy of permanency could be implemented for as many foster-care children as possible. In doing so, the project became an instrument through which policy could be optimized.

These changes also served to expand the project's influence. Rein notes that demonstration projects are successful only insofar as they can influence long-term policy (Rein, 1970). This influence may take any of three forms: (1) *spread,* in which projects are exactly duplicated elsewhere; (2) *continuity,* in which projects are continued on a more permanent basis; and (3) *spillover,* in which the project serves as a catalyst for change. At the end of the three-year period, plans were made to continue the project on a more permanent basis so that it could continue to serve special-needs children in the four-county area. In addition, the project had pointed to problems in the system that were hindering the planning of permanency for a sizable number of children, particularly those from minority backgrounds. By taking on an expanded role, the project served as a catalyst in bringing about changes in the host agencies that would optimize a child's chances for permanency.

Evaluation of Program Goals and Processes. The evaluation of the adoption project followed a utilization-focused model in which a feedback system was developed so that evaluation results could be incorporated into the decision-making processes, thus maximizing the use of evaluation findings (Patton, 1978). As Weiss (1973b) notes, evaluation results must be available for use during the course of a project if they are to have utility. Evaluation findings that are part of such a feedback process may be used to improve the program operations and, thus, the implementation of policy.

The evaluation of the adoption project was an integral part of program implementation. The evaluation had four foci: (1) measurement of official program goals; (2) description and evaluation of program activities; (3) documentation of individual cases where the data pointed to impermanency; and (4) evaluation of the coordination process through which the project was implemented, including an assessment of the impact of the project on the host agencies. Results from each component of the evaluation were periodically fed back to project staff and agency administrators. This feedback allowed staff and administrators to identify problems and to take action that would improve policy implementation. Thus, this process created the conditions under which the policy of permanency for children in foster care could be optimized.

The least useful aspect of this evaluation proved to be the measurement of official program goals. Indeed, if the evaluation had focused only on official program goals, it would have concluded that the project had much less impact than the other evaluative methods indicated it had. The evaluation of official program goals focused on:

1. Number of handicapped adoptive placements
2. Percentage of handicapped legal adoptions
3. Mean length of time in placement
4. Percentage of foster-home placements involving handicapped children that became adoptions
5. Mean number of placements
6. Percentage of families accepting handicapped children for adoption
7. Break-up of finalized adoptions

To measure these goals, a data collection system was established that ultimately produced information on the 2,000 foster-care children who were in care during the three-year project period. Each goal was measured over the three-year period and compared with baseline measures from the five-year period preceding the start-up of the project. In the case of the first two goals, adoptive placements and legal adoptions, there were increases, but comparison with baseline data showed that the increases were not as great as what had been achieved in the year immediately preceding the implementation of the project. With respect to mean length of time in care and mean number of placements, slight increases were detected during the project years, indicating a somewhat longer duration in care and more disruption in placements. However, these changes were very small and had little substantive meaning. The goal addressing the development of foster-home placements into adoptive homes was not achieved because adoptive families developed by the project were used for adoptive placements, rather than existing foster homes. Although a marked increase was demonstrated in the percentage of families accepting handicapped children for adoption, comparison with baseline data showed that this percentage had been increasing since 1970, thus inhibiting the extent to which the project could be credited with the increase. Finally, the measurement of the break-up rate of adoptions also posed problems for there were not enough cases for valid measurement. Furthermore, project staff did not feel that this goal adequately measured their work. To address this problem, a similar goal was added that looked at disruptions in adoptive placements. Project staff and administrators were able to do very little with these findings as they were submitted by the evaluators, for they did not provide sufficient information for decision making.

The evaluative findings that had more utility and that also reported a more complete picture of project impact focused on identification of problematic cases and the process of project implementation. Potentially problematic cases were identified by the evaluators through the use of a computer program that identified those children who were in the permanent custody of the agency and that listed relevant case information for each child. These lists, which were given to project staff on a periodic basis, allowed staff to monitor each agency's case load more closely, and to work with agency staff on cases where there was a need to develop permanent plans. Although not originally called for in the evaluation, these lists represented an opportunity to make systemwide data collection immediately applicable to the problem of planning permanency for foster-care children. This application of evaluative information made it more possible for the project to expand its influence with the host agencies.

The other major focus of evaluation efforts was on the process of coordination through which the project was implemented. The funding source requested that this evaluation activity augment the evaluation of official program goals so that more would be known about the process of implementing such a project. This part of the evaluation measured four areas:

1. The task accomplishment of agency and project staff with respect to project implementation
2. Emergence of unique administrative procedures and policies
3. The intergroup relations and structures of interchanges, including the integration of the project's procedures and methods into the agency's adoption programs
4. Organizational conflict

Four methods were used to collect data on these areas:

1. Participant observation, during which staff meetings were monitored and taped
2. Analysis of written documents
3. Interviews with agency administrators, agency staff, and project staff
4. Questionnaires sent to selected community groups to assess their interaction with the project

The results of this process evaluation pointed to strengths and weaknesses in the coordination model, and documented the project's impact on the system. For example, the evaluation pointed to the ways in which project staff had linked with agency workers to bring about change in the host agencies. The evaluation showed changes in workers' attitudes toward adoption of special-needs children, and a spin-off of project techniques to the agencies' regular adoption programs. In addition, this evaluation led to several recommendations for change, including a more active role for agency administrators and supervisory staff, improved communication procedures between project and non-project staff, and more staff development sessions for nonproject staff.

By delivering these evaluative findings to the funders, agency administrators, and project staff during the project, the evaluators were able to contribute to the review of policy implementation, which led to improvement during the latter half of the project term. The analysis of the coordination process also allowed the evaluation to focus on those project goals which had emerged during the course of program implementation. The coordination model evaluation was subsequently refunded for a second year to continue monitoring the coordination process and to follow progress in those areas where change had been recommended.

Summary

This chapter has argued that demonstration projects can provide an opportunity to experiment with policy implementation in ways that can lead to the optimization of policy. Conditions that create the possibility for such optimization include involvement of administrators and staff in goal setting, focus on emergent goals, use of evaluation findings during the course of policy implementation, and use of process evaluation in conjunction with goal evaluation. If each of these conditions is met during the course of policy implementation, then greater opportunity exists for optimizing policy.

References

Bennett, Carl A., and Lumsdaine, Arthur A. *Evaluation and Experiment*. New York: Academic Press, 1975.

Chestang, Leon, and Heymann, Irmgard. "Reducing the Length of Foster Care." *Social Work* 18 (January 1973):88-92.

Deutscher, Irwin. "Toward Avoiding the Goal-Trap in Evaluative Research." In *Readings in Evaluation Research*. 2d ed., edited by Francis Caro, p. 223. New York: Russell Sage, 1977.

Emlen, Arthur et al. *Freeing Children for Permanent Placement*. Vol. 1. The Barriers. Portland, Oregon: Regional Research Institute for Human Services, 1976.

Fanshel, David, and Shinn, Eugene B. *Children in Foster Care: A Longitudinal Investigation*. New York: Columbia University Press, 1978.

Gambril, Eileen D., and Wiltse, Kermit T. "Foster Care: Prescription for Change." *Public Welfare* 32 (Summer 1974):39–47.

Goldstein, Joseph; Freud, Anna; and Solnit, Albert J. *Beyond the Best Interests of the Child.* New York: The Free Press, 1973.

Jones, Martha. "Aggressive Adoption: A Program's Effect on a Child Welfare Agency." *Child Welfare* 56 (June 1977):401–408.

Knitzer, Jane, and Allen, Mary Lee. *Children without Homes: An Examination of Public Responsibility to Children in Out-of-Home Care.* Washington, D.C.: Children's Defense Fund, 1978.

Madison, Bernice, and Shapiro, Michael. "Permanent and Long-Term Foster Family Care as Planned Services." *Child Welfare* 49 (March 1970):131-136.

National Center on Child Abuse and Neglect. *Child Abuse and Neglect Reports.* Washington, D.C.: United States Department of Health, Education, and Welfare, Children's Bureau, 1979.

National Commission on Children in Need of Parents. *Who Knows? Who Cares? Forgotten Children in Foster Care.* New York: National Commission on Children in Need of Parents, 1979.

Olsen, Lenore. *Ohio District Eleven Adoption Project for Handicapped Children: Final Evaluation Report.* Cleveland, Ohio: Case Western University, Human Services Design Laboratory, 1977.

Olsen, Lenore, and Most, Shira. *Ohio District Eleven Adoption Project for Handicapped Children: Final Report of the Coordination Model Evaluation.* Cleveland, Ohio: Case Western Reserve University, Human Services Design Laboratory, 1977.

Patton, Michael Q. *Utilization-Focused Evaluation.* Beverly Hills, Calif.: Sage Publications, 1978.

Perrow, Charles. "The Analysis of Goals in Complex Organizations." *American Sociological Review* 26 (1961):855.

Pike, Victor. *Permanent Planning for Children in Foster Care: A Handbook for Social Workers.* Portland, Oregon: Regional Research Institute for Human Services, 1977.

Rein, Martin. *Social Policy.* New York: Random House, 1970, p. 140.

Shapiro, Deborah. *Agencies and Foster Children.* New York: Columbia University Press, 1976.

Sherman, Edward; Neuman, Renee; and Shyne, Ann W. *Children Adrift in Foster Care—A Study of Alternative Approaches.* New York: Child Welfare League of America, 1973.

Stein, Theodore J. "Early Intervention in Foster Care." *Public Welfare* 34 (Spring 1976):39–44.

Stein, Theodore J., and Gambril, Eileen D. "Facilitating Decision-Making in Foster Care." *Social Service Review* 51 (September 1977):502-513.

Stein, Theodore J.; Gambril, Eileen D., and Wiltse, Kermit T. *Children in Foster Homes: Achieving Continuity of Care.* New York: Preager Publishers, 1978.

Steiner, Gilbert. *The Children's Cause.* Washington, D.C.: The Brookings Institution, 1976.

Weiss, Carol. "Utilization of Evaluation: Toward Comparative Study." In *Readings in Evaluation Research.* 1st ed., edited by Francis Caro, p. 141. New York: Russel Sage, 1971.

_____. "The Politics of Impact Measurement." *Policy Studies Journal* 1 (Spring 1973a):181.

_____. "Where Politics and Evaluation Research Meet." *Evaluation* 1 (1973b):37-45.

Wiltse, Kermit T. *Current Issues and New Directions in Foster Care.* United States Department of Health, Education, and Welfare, Children's Bureau, Washington, D.C.: Government Printing Office, 1978.

12 Pursuing Policy Optimization by Evaluating Implementation: Notes on the State of the Art

James D. Sorg

A recent examination of the effect of different levels of use of individualized instruction on student achievement in reading and mathematics found curvilinear relationships among these variables (Hall and Loucks, 1977). Although the conclusions were tentative, the analysis suggested that increased use of individualized instruction led to steadily increasing mathematics scores, but that nearly the opposite resulted for reading achievement. As levels of use of individualized instruction in reading increased, reading scores first rose and then steadily declined (see figure 12-1).

From these data, we can infer that the optimal level of individualized instruction in mathematics may not have been reached. However, the optimal level of individualized instruction in reading was passed in some instances. In the case of reading, it appears to be possible to both overimplement and under-implement individualized instruction.

This illustrates that for some policies or programs it is possible to detect the optimal relationship between the extent of implementation and a policy or program's impact. By adjusting implementation, we could optimize attainment of the policy objective. To make this kind of statement or discover this type of relationship, we must collect information on implementation of policy along with information on impacts. That is, evaluation of implementation must coincide with evaluation of impact.

This chapter describes various approaches to evaluation of implementation and addresses their use for policy optimization. Evaluation of implementation is systematic data collection about the extent and form of policy implementation and analysis of that data to guide decisions about policy implementation. According to this definition, evaluation of implementation aims at producing information useful for prescription. Typically, evaluations of implementation are used: (1) to produce information useful for steering implementation as it proceeds, and (2) to produce information about the relationship between the implemented form of a policy and a policy's impact.[1]

I would like to thank Richard Brucher, Thomas Duchesneau, David Kovenock, Edward Laverty, Marcella Harnish Sorg, and Dwayne VanRheenan for comments on an earlier draft.

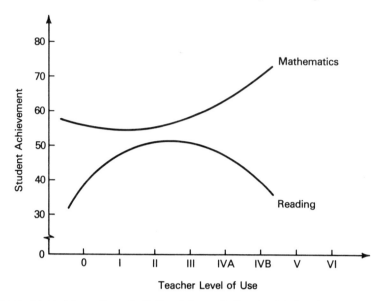

Source: Adapted from Gene E. Hall and Susan F. Loucks, "A Developmental Model for Determining Whether the Treatment is Actually Implemented," *American Educational Research Journal* 14 (Summer 1977): 273.

Figure 12-1. A Relationship between Level of Use and Goal Optimization

The theme of this chapter is that optimization of policy goals can be enhanced by evaluating the implementation of policy. By policy goal optimization I mean the attempt to maximize attainment of policy objectives subject to constraints. There are at least two points that must be noted about that definition so that we avoid misinterpretation. First, constraints are also objectives, as Majone and Wildavsky (1979, pp. 184-185) point out:

> There is no such thing as "the objective." There are always constraints as to time allowed, money permitted, procedures allowable, liberties held inviolable, and so on. That we focus our attention on a particular one, singling it out as our objective, does not mean there are not others within which we must always operate or, at least find ways to relax or overcome. Knowing only the avowed programmatic objective without being aware of other constraints is insufficient for predicting or controlling outcomes.

Thus policy optimization efforts consist not of simple pursuit of single objectives but of balancing objectives one against another.

To avoid misinterpreting the concept of policy optimization, we must also realize that policy objectives are often unstable, especially during the implementation of new policies. Policy objectives may be unstable because they may not have been clearly stated in legislation and must undergo increasing specification as they are operationalized in the field. Clearly stated objectives may change as environmental conditions change, or, through "learning by doing," as more appropriate objectives are selected. Thus, policy optimization efforts consist of pursuing objectives as we now see them, whether or not those objectives were embodied in an official policy statement.

The plan that this chapter follows is to describe two categories of implementation evaluation methods: implementation monitoring, and program documentation. Types of methods in each category will then be described along with examples of their application. The chapter will close with a preliminary assessment of the state of the art of implementation evaluation.

Types of Implementation Evaluation

The various approaches to implementation evaluation discussed in the evaluation literature can be divided into two general categories—implementation monitoring and program documentation. *Implementation monitoring* refers to information collection and analysis activities that track the processes of macroimplementation and microimplementation. Macroimplementation is a series of: "linked passages—from policy decision to government program, from program to local project adoption, from adoption to implemented local practice, and from practice to local outcomes" (Berman, 1978, p. 167). Microimplementation is the third passage in the macroimplementation process—the process by which an implementing unit adapts, and adapts to, a policy that it has been directed to implement (Berman, 1978). *Program documentation* refers to the recording of the characteristics of an implemented policy or program as part of impact evaluation (Morris and Fitz-Gibbon, 1978). In the following pages, implementation monitoring and program documentation techniques are reviewed.

Implementation Monitoring

Monitoring implementation consists of tracking the process by which a policy has been or is being operationalized by administrative agencies. Implementation monitoring may be undertaken for various reasons:

> To detect difficulties that arise in particular stages of a policy's implementation, as when a demonstration project is geared up for widespread implementation (Boruch and Wortman, 1979, p. 332).

> To monitor variation when variation in the implemented form of the programs is intentional, as in the follow-through planned variation experiments (Morris and Fitz-Gibbon, 1978, p. 32).

To track the adaptation of policies as they progress through the passages of the implementation process. A policy may be adapted (1) as the authoritative policy statement is converted to a government program, (2) as the program is adopted by lower-level agencies (adaptation where is called *slippage*), and (3) during microimplementation as the local agency grapples with its implementation (adaptation at this passage is termed *mutation*) (Berman, 1978, p. 171).

To identify the institutional characteristics of a policy system that may be manipulated to optimize policy objectives (Chadwin et al., 1977).

To assure that the official description of the program reflects how the program is actually being conducted (Morris and Fitz-Gibbon, 1978, p. 19).

To measure coverage and bias among program participants. Coverage refers to the "extent to which a program enjoys widespread target population participation ... Bias is the extent to which subgroups of the designated target population ... participate" (Rossi, Freeman, and Wright, 1979, p. 124).

Macroimplementation Monitoring. Macroimplementation monitoring consists of tracing the process by which a policy progresses from legislation (or other mandate) to action in order to determine (1) what is being implemented, (2) why it is taking a particular form, and (3) what actions can be taken to influence implementation.

One method of macroimplementation will be discussed here—the U.S. Government Accounting Office's (GAO) recommended procedure for evaluating implementation. The procedure is intended to aid Congress in carrying out oversight by providing answers to the following questions:

1. Has the executive branch initiated implementation of the program?
2. Has the responsible executive agency developed, designed, and established the program?
3. Are specific program activities and operations being carried out at the field or operating level of the program?
4. Can the operating program be evaluated, and can congressional oversight questions be answered using agreed on measurements and comparisons within acceptable limits of time, cost, and precision? (GAO, 1977, p. iii)

The GAO recommends that Congress monitor implementation as it occurs rather than checking a program for conformity with congressional intent after it has been implemented. This recommendation is based on an understanding that the implementation effort itself often changes the goals, resources, and strategies that Congress originally had intended. In most cases, Congress

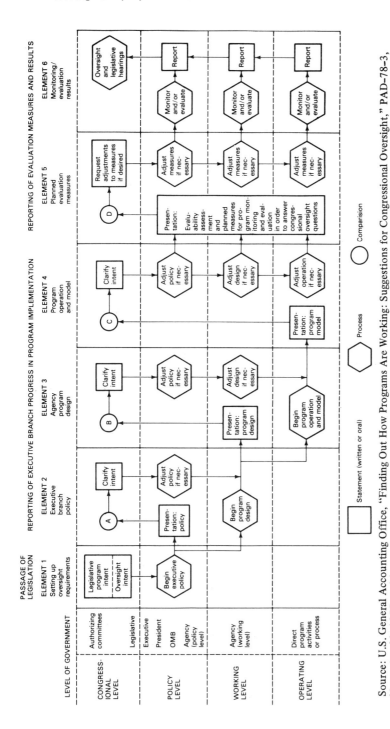

Figure 12-2. Flow Diagram of the Government Accounting Office's Suggested Oversight Process

Source: U.S. General Accounting Office, "Finding Out How Programs Are Working: Suggestions for Congressional Oversight," PAD-78-3, November 22, 1977, p. 24.

and other legislative bodies cannot state clear goals, specify administrative structures, or designate implementation strategies when laws are formulated. In fact, it may be important for Congress to avoid overspecifying "legislative language or goals when knowledge or political reality does not permit" (GAO, 1977, p. 10).

Given that ambiguous language is frequently necessary at early stages of the policy process, legislative bodies and administrative policymakers will have to carefully monitor implementation so that as the implemented form of the policy evolves, it will reflect legislative intent. The GAO's proposal for a macroimplementation monitoring technique could aid policy optimization efforts by helping to maintain a correspondence between the objectives that implementors attempt to optimize in the field and those objectives intended for optimization by legislative policymakers. When implementation efforts stray from pursuit of objectives intended by legislators or when official statements of policy intention lag behind the reality of implemented policy, macroimplementation monitoring can provide the information needed to close the gap.

The GAO's suggested procedure is depicted in figure 12-2 and described in table 12-1. The process consists of a sequence of steps beginning with congressional expression of legislative and oversight intentions. As the executive branch develops a strategy for carrying out the policy, designs the operating program, and implements the program, it informs relevant committees and congressmen of these efforts. Congress, in turn, clarifies its intent and asks for any needed program adjustments. Both branches participate in formulating the criteria and research plans that will guide evaluation of the program.

The costs of this proposed oversight procedure would be high, although the procedure would not be invoked in full for every program. The principal benefits of the procedure, according to the GAO, would be the avoidance of costly evaluation studies that are misdirected and hence unused because they are commissioned without full understanding of the implemented form of the policy or preferred evaluation criteria.

Microimplementation Monitoring. Microimplementation monitoring consists of collecting information to describe the form a policy has taken in various implementing jurisdictions in order to determine (1) the extent of compliance, (2) the adaptation a policy has undergone as it has been operationalized, (3) the reasons for noncompliance or adaptation, and (4) manipulatable aspects of implementation that can be used to alter the rate and direction of the process in pursuit of policy goal optimization.

If an intensive and extensive knowledge base underlies policymaking in a particular area, then policymakers will know *how* to optimize policy goals. If there is consensus about the objectives of the policy, policymakers will know *which* objectives to optimize. In such a case, the most useful information about

Table 12-1

Suggested Oversight Process Elements; Portion of Oversight Feedback Loop

Element Number	Implementation of a Program	Feedback of Information	Congressional Response/Requirements
1	n/a	n/a	Include a statement of legislative and oversight intent in the enabling act or accompanying reports
2	Formulation of executive-branch policy and strategy for carrying out the enabling act's intent	Presentation of executive-branch policy	(Point A) Clarify intent and request policy adjustments if desired
3	Planning, design, and development of an operating program by agency working level	Presentation of agency progress in program design	(Point B) Clarify intent and request policy and/or program design adjustments if desired
4	Establishment and initial execution of an operating program; model the actual program operation	Presentation of agency model of the operating program	(Point C) Clarify intent and request policy, program design, and/or program operation adjustments if desired
5	Perform evaluability assessment and develop planned evaluation measures	Presentation of evaluability assessment and planned evaluation measures	(Point D) Request adjustments to planned evaluation measures if desired
6	Conduct program evaluations and monitoring	Report results of the program evaluations and monitoring	Assess program results; amend, extend, or terminate enabling act; develop and include a new statement of legislative intent if appropriate

Source: From U.S. General Accounting Office, "Finding Out How Programs Are Working: Suggestions for Congressional Oversight," PAD-78-3, November 22, 1977, p. 23.

implementation may be the extent of deviation of implemented programs from policy intentions. With this knowledge, policymakers can bring recalcitrant programs back on the path to policy optimization. Although there are relatively few policy areas with a well-developed knowledge base and consensus about which objectives to optimize, an implementation monitoring technique called compliance auditing, which focuses on detecting deviation from policy intentions, is often employed.

Compliance Audits. Compliance audits most often take the form of discrepancy evaluations (Provus, 1971). The objective of the audit is to determine the extent of conformity with policy standards and objectives. An example of a compliance audit is the substitute-care policy compliance study undertaken in 1977 by the Maine Department of Human Services (1977). This study examined the degree and consistency of the department's substitute-care policies and procedures as they were implemented by the department's regional offices. The method employed was a systematic survey of case records to discover: (1) the level of compliance with the basic requirements as stated in the Approved Policy Statement (APS) or policy memoranda, (2) extent of noncompliance, and (3) baseline data related to the current status of the substitute care program (Maine Department of Human Services, 1977, p. 3).

Compliance audits may be quite useful for monitoring administration of routine and stable policies. However, they may not be appropriate for monitoring the implementation of new policies, or in situations where it is recognized that (1) the knowledge base underlying policy is scant, (2) the policy environment is turbulent, or (3) the policy goals to be optimized are not agreed on, are vaguely stated, or are shifting. In these policy areas, information that implementation is deviating from policy intentions is not very helpful. Those managing implementation need information about *how* policy is being operationalized by implementors, and how policy *should be* operationalized in order to optimize policy objectives.

Mapping Adaptations. Compliance audits assume a fixed policy; however, it appears that most policies and programs undergo adaptation as they are put in place (Berman and McLaughlin, 1974; Eveland, Rogers, and Klepper, 1977; Majone and Wildavsky, 1979; Larsen and Agarwala-Rogers, 1977). Some students of policy implementation believe that this adaptation is necessary for effective implementation of social-service policies (Berman, 1978; Johnson and O'Connor, 1979). Given that adaptation occurs, mapping the resultant configurations of the policy will be of use to program managers and policymakers who wish to know about or influence the process.

A promising method for mapping adaptations of policies is being developed by Hall and Loucks (1978). The method is based on the concept of innovation configurations, which are "the operational patterns of the innovation that result from selection and use of different innovation component variations" (p. 9).

Hall and Loucks view a program or policy as a set of components or characteristics from which an implementor may choose those components which fit his situation, adapt other components, and reject still others. "How the component variations are selected, how they are organized, and the way they are used by the actors result in different operational forms of the innovation or different innovation configurations" (Hall and Loucks, 1978, p. 10).

Hall and Loucks's method for determining policy innovation configurations consists of: (1) interviewing policymakers to determine their views of the essential components of the policy, (2) interviewing and observing a small number of implementors to discover the components of the policy as they have operationalized it, (3) from the two sets of interviews, preparing a formal interview guide to discover the variant components of the policy, and interviewing a large number of implementors, (4) constructing a checklist of policy components and completing it for each (or a sample) implementor, and (5) analyzing the checklist results to determine the dominant configurations of the implemented policy (adapted from Hall and Loucks, 1978, p. 24). This method would provide policymakers with a map of the various operational forms of a policy.

Explaining Variation. Beyond describing the variation in operational forms of policy, we need to attempt to explain why the variation occurs. Such evaluations of implementation could result in recommendations about reduction of variations or the opposite. An evaluation of the implementation of a federal job-based alcoholism policy resulted in advice about how to reduce variation in the policy's implementation. Trice, Beyer, and Hunt (1978) concluded that an alcoholism policy would have been implemented more consistently and extensively if: (1) lower-level managers had been involved in operationalizing the policy, (2) information about the policy had been diffused more effectively, and (3) resources for implementation had been available.

On the other hand, an evaluation of implementation may conclude that variations in the operational configuration or extent of implementation are desirable. Johnson and O'Connor (1979) examined compliance with departmental regulations by income-maintenance and social-services workers in the Pennsylvania Department of Public Welfare. They went beyond measuring deviation from regulations to attempt to explain why deviation occurred. They found that a large number of workers frequently did not comply with central administration policy regulations when they seemed to conflict with their own definition of being a responsible public official. Johnson and O'Connor accounted for this noncompliance by examining the influence of the following variables on compliance: perceived usefulness of communications about policy from central administration, perceived consistency of policy communications, sufficiency of time to read regulations, perception of how realistic regulations are, perception of whether central administration seriously expects regulations to be carried out, and perception of whether central administrators know enough to make good decisions.

Johnson and O'Connor concluded "that while central administration policy often is not implemented in the sense of following the regulations, workers who fail to implement it seem to be servicing clients in ways that many . . . believe are appropriate to welfare system objectives" (p. 202).

As Johnson and O'Connor point out, two possible strategies can be derived from their research. First, one could tighten control by resolving communications problems, providing resources, and, through hiring and incentives, assure willingness to comply. Second, one could loosen the reigns by giving workers more varied responsibility for their cases, more flexibility in interpreting policy, and broadly written rather than detailed central-level policy. The researchers favor the latter because they believe that clients will be better served as a result. However, they hasten to add that they have no data to support this last conclusion.

One additional conclusion Johnson and O'Connor draw should be mentioned. "Research should be directed at policy decisions made at the operating level and their consequences, rather than looking for evidence of noncompliant behavior which then suggests better organizational control systems" (p. 208). The creators of another method of implementation evaluation, called institutional analysis, seem to agree with Johnson and O'Connor that effective client service should be highly valued, but they would advocate pursuit of other, sometimes conflicting values, as well.

> The effort to improve implementation assumes as values that federal officials (or lower-level officials) acting legally and constitutionally should be obeyed, and that public agencies should live up to norms of effectiveness and efficiency. (Mead, 1977, p. 24)

Institutional analysis is a method of implementation evaluation to be used to explain reasons for variations in the operational form of policies and to prescribe actions to be taken to further implementation. The method examines the relationship between the administrative and political structure of programs and program performance. Program performance is defined in terms of program output or effort rather than impact; in terms of services delivered, rather than beneficial changes in client characteristics. Program efficiency may also be examined, again, in light of administrative and political factors affecting costs.

Institutional analysis aspires to base itself on economic, organization, and political theory in the effort to explain program performance. Each of these explains a slightly different aspect. Economic theory explains incentives "that may encourage or inhibit implementation. Organization theory explicates some of the basic weaknesses of large bureaucracies such as their communication and coordination problems. Political theory, especially interest group theory, helps explain the ability of provider groups to "capture" the implementation of programs" (Mead, 1979, p. 27).

Mead has applied institutional analysis to the Medicare program to try to discover why a program that was intended to provide adequate care to its client population at a reasonable cost provides instead inadequate care at unreasonable cost (Mead, 1977). Institutional analysis has also been applied to a study of the U.S. Employment Service (Chadwin et al., 1977) and several other programs (see Mead, 1979, p. 27).

Institutional analysis, as do the other microimplementation monitoring methods, eschews examination of the relationship between the implemented form of a program and its effectiveness. Thus, these studies do not themselves provide data on the linkage between implemented policy and policy goal optimization. That is the province of policy impact evaluation. However, the information on implementation provided by microimplementation monitoring, when combined with the data on policy effectiveness from impact evaluation, is useful for steering policy implementation efforts in the direction of goal optimization.

Program Documentation

There are four reasons that implementation evaluation, as program documentation, is an important component of impact evaluation. First, before we invest time and money in an evaluation of impact, we should know *that* the program in question has been implemented. Second, it is essential to the design of a valid impact evaluation that we know *how* the program has been implemented. That is, data from implementation evaluations should guide design of impact evaluations. Third, we must document program implementation in order to avoid misinterpretation of impact evaluation results. Finally, we must document program implementation in search of causal relationships between program elements and observed effects. If causal relationships can be discovered, it may be possible to manipulate implementation to optimize policy goals.

Guiding the Design of Impact Evaluations. Although there have been cases of impact evaluations conducted on programs that have not been implemented at all (Patton, 1978, pp. 149-150), it is more likely that impact evaluations not guided by information about program implementation will be poorly designed and less than useful for policymakers and program managers. Impact evaluations designed without information on implementation will, since policies and programs usually undergo change as they are applied, evaluate not the implemented program but an abstract concept that may or may not have been operationalized in the field.

The GAO has identified specific areas of impact evaluation design that must be informed by knowledge about implementation:

> Knowledge of how the actual activities are being carried out is needed to determine what can be measured, what those measurements would be, how much they would cost, where they would be obtained, and how reliable and valid they would be in describing a program's activities, processes, outcomes, impacts, and effectiveness in meeting the legislative intent. (GAO, 1977, p. 4)

Implementation evaluation as a precursor of impact evaluation is important for another reason. Several evaluators note that it is essential to know whether the goals and procedures of a program have stabilized in order to avoid premature impact evaluations (Trice, Beyer, and Hunt, 1978, p. 449; Boruch and Wortman, 1979, p. 331). Morris and Fitz-Gibbon note that impact evaluation should not proceed until "the program has had sufficient time to correct problems and function smoothly" (1978, p. 14). However, they go on to say that:

> Unfortunately, funding agencies often request summative reports at a time in the life of a program when considerable variation still exists. When this happens, the summative evaluator should note that several *different* program renditions are being evaluated. He should describe each of these, *and report results separately*, making comparisons where possible. (pp. 33–34, italics in original)

Actually, since many programs will be characterized by considerable variation after they have stabilized, Morris and Fitz-Gibbon's advice has general applicability.

Avoiding Misinterpretation of Results. We must know about the implemented form that a program takes at various sites in order to accurately interpret the results of impact evaluations. "An evaluation that ignores implementation will throw together results from sites where the program has been conscientiously installed with those from places which might have decided 'Let's not and say we did'" (Morris and Fitz-Gibbon, 1978, p. 11).

Hall and Loucks (1977) provide an illustration of a program that had been in effect for two to three years. They report a considerable variation in the extent of implementation of individualized instruction by teachers in schools that were participating in an Individualized Guided Education (IGE) program. Some used individualized instruction very infrequently, others somewhat more. This is a good example of variation in implementation; however, another finding is more striking. In a comparison of teachers in schools that participated in the program (IGE schools) with teachers from schools that were not involved (non-IGE-schools) Hall and Loucks found that "a sizeable number of IGE school teachers *were not* in fact individualizing, and many of the teachers in the non-IGE schools *were* individualizing their instruction!" (p. 269, italics in original). They point out how misleading it would be to draw conclusions about the effectiveness of IGE in a comparison with this set of non-IGE schools. One cannot assume that the policy or program has been implemented in the treatment group and is absent in the control group; one must document implementation to demonstrate this.

Searching for Causal Relationships. The most obvious application of implementation evaluation in pursuit of policy goal optimization is in detecting causal relationships between implemented program components and observed program impacts. Impact evaluations are undertaken to search for such relationships. Does program x produce the observed changes in client characteristics, or is there an alternative explanation for those observed changes? If we are to draw conclusions about program effectiveness beyond particular evaluated sites, we must describe the characteristics of program x that are causally linked to client characteristics. Program documentation provides such descriptions.

Since adaptation of policies and programs during implementation is so common, impact evaluations should focus on documenting the links between the various implemented forms of a policy and policy impacts. In other words, impact evaluations should attempt to explain variations in policy optimization with reference to documented variations in the operational configuration of the policy. In this way we learn which of the implemented versions of the policy are most effective, and can give policymakers information about how far we can deviate from an ideal model and still have intended effects (Patton, 1978, p. 162). That is, we should aim at giving policymakers information about the varying effects of program x, x', and x''.

The analysis of the relationship between extent of implementation of individualized instruction and reading and mathematics achievement described at the beginning of this chapter provides very useful information for policy optimization. With information on variation in extent of implementation and variation in effectiveness, we could, hypothetically, devise an ideal model (x) for a program of individualized instruction in reading and mathematics. By monitoring implementation, we could determine deviation from the ideal model. We may determine that if instruction deviated from the ideal model but stayed within certain upper and lower bounds (x'), the program would be reasonably effective. An instructional program that exceeded those bounds (x'') would be expected to be ineffective.

This kind of analysis indicates that in some cases it may be possible to discover the optimal relationship between extent of implementation of a policy, program, or technique and the desired level of impact. However, we have learned enough about the difficulties of implementation to avoid being overly optimistic about our ability to move from this kind of analysis to the fine-tuning of policy.

The State of the Art of Implementation Evaluation

An assessment of the state of the art of implementation evaluation should answer these questions: (1) What is the theoretical basis for the method? (2) Is the method replicable? (3) Is the method codified or codifiable? (4) Do the benefits of its application outweigh its costs? Because it may be premature to address these criteria in a rigorous way, the following comments will be general rather than specific.

The theoretical bases underlying implementation evaluation are generally weak. Two bodies of theory are relevant to this assessment: the substantive theory of the policy being evaluated (for example, the theory underlying crime prevention or regional economic development), and the theory of policy implementation itself. Several of the examples of implementation evaluation described in this chapter drew on conceptual frameworks to explain implementation failure (see Trice, Beyer, and Hunt, 1978; Johnson and O'Connor, 1979; and Mead, 1977, 1979). But the sources relied on were no more than conceptual frameworks. A full theory (see Berman, 1978) of policy implementation does not yet exist. Moreover, there is great variability in the adequacy of many of the theories or conceptual frameworks that would inform policymaking in substantive policy areas like criminal justice or health.

Second, we do not have enough experience with most of the forms of implementation evaluation to assess the extent to which a particular technique is a replicable methodology. For what types of policies is a method useful? Can it be used for evaluating implementation of regulatory, distributive, and redistributive policies? Within a particular policy type, can the method be used in roughly the same way in more than one instance? What kinds of adaptations are necessary?

Third, if methods are not replicable, then they are not easily transmitted to other policy analysts who would like to employ them. Morris and Fitz-Gibbon (1978) have codified a technique for program documentation of education programs. But to my knowledge, this is the only example of a codified method of program documentation. Although the list of impact evaluations that include program documentation is growing (see Fullan and Pomfret, 1977; Boruch and Wortman, 1979), there is little guidance outside the field of education about how to document implementation. There is a similar lack of method codification of implementation monitoring. GAO's oversight procedure is fairly explicit, but to my knowledge, not yet tested. Microimplementation monitoring techniques are still in the developmental stages.

Finally, the crucial question about implementation evaluation concerns the value of the information such studies produce relative to their cost. This question is unanswered and may be no easier to answer than questions about the costs and benefits of other policy analysis methods.

Although implementation evaluation methods do not meet these criteria at this time, their application will be enhanced if theoretical foundation, replicability, codification, and cost-benefit criteria are considered as they are further developed.

Conclusion

Implementation evaluation is a new endeavor of policy analysts that may be very useful for policy goal optimization. Macroimplementation monitoring can help guide the translation of policy concepts into effective operational programs. Microimplementation monitoring is useful for describing variation in operational programs and discovering reasons for that variation. Program documentation as a precursor of program impact evaluation prevents the miscarriage of such evaluations. Program documentation as a component of program impact evaluation is indispensable in the search for links between the implemented form of programs and program effects.

Note

1. Evaluation of implementation is distinguishable from implementation feasibility analysis. The latter technique is applied prior to policy adoption and focuses on predicting obstacles to implementation and recommending changes in policy design to avoid or overcome them. Evaluation of implementation occurs during and/or after the implementation of policy.

References

Berman, Paul. "The Study of Macro- and Micro-Implementation." *Public Policy* 26 (Spring 1978):157–184.

Berman, Paul, and McLaughlin, Milbrey. *Federal Programs Supporting Educational Change*. Vol. 4. Santa Monica, Calif.: Rand, 1974.

Boruch, Robert F., and Wortman, Paul M. "Implications of Educational Evaluation for Evaluation Policy." In *Review of Research in Education*, edited by David C. Berliner, pp. 303–363. No. 7, American Educational Research Association, 1979.

Chadwin, Mark Lincoln; Mitchell, John J.; Hargrove, Erwin C.; and Mead, Lawrence M. "The Employment Service: An Institutional Analysis." Employment and Training Administration, Department of Labor, R & D Monograph 51, 1977.

Eveland, J.D.; Rogers, Everett M.; and Klepper, Constance. *The Innovation Process in Public Organizations*. Ann Arbor, Mich.: University of Michigan, 1977.

Fullan, Michael, and Pomfret, Alan. "Research on Curriculum and Instruction Implementation." *Review of Educational Research* 47 (1977):335–397.

Hall, Gene E., and Loucks, Susan F. "A Developmental Model for Determining Whether the Treatment Is Actually Implemented." *American Educational Research Journal* 14 (Summer 1977):263–276.

_____. *Innovation Configurations: Analyzing the Adaptations of Innovations*. Austin, Texas: R & D Center for Teacher Education, University of Texas, 1978).

Johnson, Ronald W., and O'Connor, Robert E. "Intraagency Limitations on Policy Implementation." *Administration and Society* 11 (August 1979): 193–215.

Larsen, Judith, and Agarwala-Rogers, Rekha. "Reinvention of Innovative Ideas: Modified? Adopted? None of the Above." *Evaluation* 4(1977):136-140.

Maine Department of Human Services, Bureau of Resource Development. "An Evaluation of Substitute Care Policy/Procedure." Augusta, Maine, July, 1977.

Majone, Giandomencio, and Wildavsky, Aaron. "Implementation as Evolution." In *Policy Studies Review Annual*. Vol. 2. Edited by Howard E. Freeman. Beverly Hills, Calif.: Sage Publications, 1979.

Mead, Lawrence M. *Institutional Analysis: An Approach to Implementation Problems in Medicaid.* Washington, D.C.: The Urban Institute, 1977.

_____. "Institutional Analysis for State and Local Government." *Public Administration Review* 39 (January/February 1979):26-30.

Morris, Lynn Lyons, and Fitz-Gibbon, Carol Taylor. *How to Measure Program Implementation.* Beverly Hills, Calif.: Sage Publications, 1978.

Patton, Michael Q. *Utilization-Focused Evaluation.* Beverly Hills, Calif.: Sage Publications, 1978.

Provus, Malcolm. *Discrepancy Evaluation for Educational Program Improvement and Assessment.* Berkeley, Calif.: McCutchan, 1971.

Rossi, Peter H.; Freeman, Howard E.; and Wright, Sonia R. *Evaluation: A Systematic Approach.* Beverly Hills, Calif.: Sage Publications, 1979. Chap. 4.

Trice, Harrison M.; Beyer, Janice M.; and Hunt, Richard E. "Evaluating Implementation of a Job-Based Alcoholism Policy." *Journal of Studies on Alcohol* 39(1978):448-465.

U.S. General Accounting Office. "Finding Out How Programs Are Working: Suggestions for Congressional Oversight." PAD-78-3, November 22, 1977.

Indexes

Name Index

Subject Index

List of Contributors

Peter A. Easton has served for several years as a consultant in educational evaluation and planning in West Africa and has been a research associate in the evaluation of the Florida Linkage System.

Garrett R. Foster is professor of educational research and evaluation in the College of Education of the Florida State University (Department of Educational Research, Development, and Foundations).

James A. Goodrich is assistant professor of public administration in the School of Business and Public Administration, University of the Pacific, Stockton, California.

Gustav Koehler is a principal consultant with California Technical Assistance Associates, a management consulting firm in Sacramento, California.

Guenther Kress is a principal consultant with California Technical Associates and adjunct professor of political science at the University of Southern California.

Beryce W. MacLellan is senior mental health advisor in the Human Resources Division of the U.S. General Accounting Office.

Michael C. Musheno is director of the Center for Criminal Justice Studies and associate professor of criminal justice and public affairs at Arizona State University.

Robert T. Nakamura is assistant professor of government at Dartmouth College.

Lenore Olsen is research director for the Council for Community Services, Inc., Providence, Rhode Island.

Dianne M. Pinderhughes is assistant professor of government at Dartmouth College.

George R. Rawson is assistant professor of political science at the University of New Orleans.

Elaine B. Sharp is research associate at the Center for Public Affairs and assistant professor of political science at The University of Kansas.

167

James D. Sorg is assistant professor of political science at the University of Maine.

J. Fred Springer is a senior consultant with the California legislature and adjunct professor at the University of Southern California.

John Clayton Thomas is assistant professor of political science and acting director of the Master's Program in Public Administration at Texas Christian University in Fort Worth.

About the Editors

Dennis J. Palumbo is director of the Center for Public Affairs and professor of political science at The University of Kansas. He has held a number of administrative positions and has taught at several universities, including the Universities of Pennsylvania, Hawaii, and Indiana, Michigan State University, and City University of New York. Professor Palumbo is the author of and contributor to several books; his most recent book, written with James Levine and Michael Musheno, is *Criminal Justice: A Public Policy Approach*. He has published numerous articles and monographs and has been a consultant with state and local government agencies in New York, Indiana, Kansas, Oklahoma, Missouri, and Hawaii.

Marvin A. Harder is professor of political science and director of the Capitol Complex Center of The University of Kansas. He was formerly special assistant to the governor of Kansas for policy review and coordination and is the author of *The Kansas Legislature* and *The Legislature as an Organization*. Professor Harder is currently writing a case study of a gubernatorial administration that will focus on policy development and implementation.